DATE DUE

Real-World STEM: Securing Cyberspace

Other titles in the *Real-World STEM* series include:

Real-World STEM: Securing Cyberspace

Bradley Steffens

ReferencePoint Press®

San Diego, CA

LIBRARY OF CONGRESS CATALOGING-IN-PUBLICATION DATA

Name: Steffens, Bradley, 1955– author.
Title: Real-World STEM: Securing Cyberspace/by Bradley Steffens.
Description: San Diego, CA: ReferencePoint Press, Inc., 2018. | Series:
  Real-World STEM series | Includes bibliographical references and index. |
  Audience: Grade 9–12.
Identifiers: LCCN 2017011706 (print) | LCCN 2017027492 (ebook) | ISBN
  9781682822500 (eBook) | ISBN 9781682822494 (hardback)
Subjects: LCSH: Computer security—Juvenile literature. |
  Cyberspace—Juvenile literature.
Classification: LCC QA76.9.A25 (ebook) | LCC QA76.9.A25 S745 2018 (print) |
  DDC 005.8—dc23
LC record available at https://lccn.loc.gov/2017011706

CONTENTS

Great Engineering Achievements

 **Electrification**
Vast networks of electricity provide power for the developed world.

 Automobile
Revolutionary manufacturing practices made cars more reliable and affordable, and the automobile became the world's major mode of transportation.

3 Airplane
Flying made the world accessible, spurring globalization on a grand scale.

Water Supply and Distribution
Engineered systems prevent the spread of disease, increasing life expectancy.

 **5 Electronics**
First with vacuum tubes and later with transistors, electronic circuits underlie nearly all modern technologies.

 Radio and Television
These two devices dramatically changed the way the world receives information and entertainment.

 Agricultural Mechanization
Numerous agricultural innovations led to a vastly larger, safer, and less costly food supply.

Computers
Computers are now at the heart of countless operations and systems that impact people's lives.

 8

 9 Telephone
The telephone changed the way the world communicates personally and in business.

 **10 Air Conditioning and Refrigeration**
Beyond providing convenience, these innovations extend the shelf life of food and medicines, protect electronics, and play an important role in health care delivery.

Highways

Forty-four thousand miles of US highways enable personal travel and the wide distribution of goods.

Spacecraft

Going to outer space vastly expanded humanity's horizons and resulted in the development of more than sixty thousand new products on Earth.

Internet

The Internet provides a global information and communications system of unparalleled access.

13

Imaging

Numerous imaging tools and technologies have revolutionized medical diagnostics.

Household Appliances

These devices have eliminated many strenuous and laborious tasks.

15 **14**

Health Technologies

From artificial implants to the mass production of antibiotics, these technologies have led to vast health improvements.

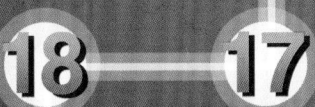

16

Laser and Fiber Optics

Their applications are wide and varied, including almost simultaneous worldwide communications, noninvasive surgery, and point-of-sale scanners.

Petroleum and Petrochemical Technologies

These technologies provided the fuel that energized the twentieth century.

18 **17**

Nuclear Technologies

From splitting the atom came a new source of electric power.

19

High-Performance Materials

They are lighter, stronger, and more adaptable than ever before.

20

Source: Wm. A. Wulf, "Great Achievements and Grand Challenges," National Academy of Engineering, *The Bridge*, Fall/Winter 2000. www.nae.edu.

A Growing Concern

"There was a systematic lack of cybersecurity competence across the DNC [Democratic National Committee] and the [Hillary] Clinton campaign."

—Kaveh Waddell, reporter for the *Atlantic*

Kaveh Waddell, "Why Some People Think a Typo Cost Clinton the Election," *Atlantic*, December 16, 2016. www.theatlantic.com.

Hacking—the process of gaining access to computer systems and files without permission—and cybersecurity—the process used to prevent hacking—have been in the news regularly in recent years. One notable hacking incident occurred during the US presidential campaign of 2016. In July of that year, WikiLeaks, an international nonprofit organization that publishes news leaks and classified information from various sources, released twenty thousand e-mails obtained by hacking into the computers of the Democratic National Committee (DNC). The e-mails proved extremely embarrassing to the DNC because they suggested that the organization had favored former secretary of state Hillary Clinton over her rival for the Democratic presidential nomination, Vermont senator Bernie Sanders (Clinton won the Democratic nomination). "Top officials at the Democratic National Committee criticized and mocked Senator Bernie Sanders of Vermont during the primary campaign, even though the organization publicly insisted that it was neutral in the race, according to committee emails made public on Friday by WikiLeaks,"[1] states an article in the *New York Times*. After the e-mails became public, DNC chair Debbie Wasserman Schultz resigned. Then in October, just weeks before the election, WikiLeaks released thousands of e-mails hacked from the account of Clinton's campaign manager, John Podesta. These e-mails were even more damaging than the DNC e-mails. They appeared to show that Clinton held private beliefs contrary to her public positions, suggesting to some that she was not honest and trustworthy.

Although Clinton won the popular vote in the November 8 election, she narrowly lost a few key states, giving an Electoral College win to her Republican opponent, Donald Trump. The margins of victory were so small in some states that many analysts believe the hacked e-mails may have been the deciding factor in the election's outcome. "The . . . email leaks likely harmed Clinton's chances of winning the presidency,"[2] writes Kaveh Waddell of the *Atlantic*. Harry Enten, a senior political writer and analyst for the polling organization FiveThirtyEight, agreed. "The evidence suggests Wikileaks is among the factors that might have contributed to her loss,"[3] says Enten.

Foreign Hackers and the Election ■

The hacking scandal did not end with the election. One month later, the *Washington Post* reported that US intelligence agencies

The November 8, 2016, US presidential election between Donald Trump and Hillary Clinton (shown) was so close that many thought the preelection hack of the Democratic National Committee's computers may have been a significant factor in the election's outcome.

had concluded that people with connections to the Russian government had provided WikiLeaks with the hacked e-mails. Based on these intelligence reports, then-president Barack Obama placed sanctions on four Russian individuals and five Russian entities for interfering with the election. He also ordered thirty-five Russian diplomats to leave the country. "Russia's cyberactivities were intended to influence the election, erode faith in US democratic institutions, sow doubt about the integrity of our electoral process, and undermine confidence in the institutions of the US government," declared a joint statement of the White House and the Treasury Department. "These actions are unacceptable and will not be tolerated."[4] In a press conference one week later, Obama described the election hack as part of a larger threat that must be met with new and effective countermeasures:

> In this new cyber age, we're going to have to make sure that we continually work to find the right balance of accountability and openness and transparency that is the hallmark of our democracy. But also recognize that there are adversaries and bad actors out there who want to use that same openness in ways that hurt us, whether that's in trying to commit financial crimes or trying to commit acts of terrorism or folks who want to interfere with our elections. And we're going to have to continually build the kind of architecture to make sure our—the best of our democracy is preserved.[5]

As Obama pointed out, hackers have carried out cyberattacks on a wide range of targets for a variety of reasons, including political activism, terrorism, and greed. The 2016 presidential election hack showed how political activists, sometimes called hacktivists, use hacking to further their ends. An example of terrorist activism occurred in 2014, when terrorists hacked into the computer systems of a South Korean nuclear power plant in an effort to destroy the nuclear reactor and cause the release of radioactive material. Hacking to get money is especially common. In 2015 hackers broke into the Internal Revenue Service (IRS) computer system, accessed seven hundred thousand taxpayer accounts, and filed fake tax returns that caused nearly $50 million in fraudulent refunds to be deposited into the hackers' bank accounts. In 2016 the social networking website Myspace confirmed that hackers had stolen more than 427 million of its user passwords. That same year, Yahoo! confirmed that in 2013 hackers had gained access to more than 1 billion Yahoo! user records, including names, telephone numbers, birth dates, passwords, and security questions that could be used to reset a password. In both cases, the hackers offered the stolen data for sale to other hackers, who could then use the information to steal money from online accounts.

A Loss of Confidence ■

With hacking becoming so common, many people are losing confidence in doing business on the Internet. According to a 2015 study by the National Telecommunications and Information Administration, half of all Americans are using the Internet less than they used to, due to fears about security and privacy. In his keynote address to the Black Hat USA 2016 cybersecurity conference, noted security researcher Dan Kaminsky called for a federal agency devoted to cybersecurity issues that can "create engineering solutions to the real-world security problems that we have." He added, "It can't just be two guys. I need a pile of nerds to be able to work on this for ten years. We can support health and energy and roads and cars, but somehow we can't support the thing that is driving our economy right now? That's crazy."[6]

Because of widespread hacking, cybersecurity has become a top priority for businesses and government. Many organizations are hiring highly trained professionals known as cybersecurity analysts to protect their computer networks, databases, and operations from cyberattacks. They also are investing in special software designed to prevent hackers from gaining access to their computer systems. Some organizations are moving their financial operations to remote computer networks, known as the cloud, to limit access to their sensitive data. According to the research firm MarketsandMarkets, spending on the cybersecurity industry will grow more than 10 percent a year for the next few years, surpassing $200 billion worldwide by 2021.

CHAPTER 1

CURRENT STATUS: Layers of Cybersecurity Defense

"We need to go ahead and get the Internet fixed or risk losing this engine of beauty."

—Dan Kaminsky, keynote speaker at Black Hat USA 2016 cybersecurity conference

Quoted in Sheera Frenkel, "Cybersecurity Is Broken and the Hacks Are Going to Just Keep Coming," BuzzFeed, August 20, 2016. www.buzzfeed.com.

Hackers cannot gain access to a private computer network, database, or individual computer files simply by clicking on a link or an icon, the way an authorized user can. Hackers must defeat a variety of security measures designed to prevent them from accessing the computer system and the data it contains. These measures include software programs known as firewalls, user account access controls such as passwords, and intrusion detection systems that monitor computer systems, looking for specific behaviors known to be practiced by hackers. These security measures work well most of the time, but hackers are continually searching for ways to defeat them.

Firewalls ■

A firewall is a software application that examines data being sent between computers over electronic networks. To travel over electronic networks, digital data is arranged into small groups, known as packets. In addition to the data being sent, a packet also contains the delivery address for the data and information about the sender. This information is known as control information. Firewall software inspects the control information of the incoming data packets before allowing them to pass through to their destination. Some firewalls examine the entire packet to see what kind of data it contains. If the packet does not conform to the software's security rules, it is not allowed to pass through the firewall.

There are two basic kinds of firewalls. One kind of firewall serves as a barrier between a trusted network, such as an organization's own local area network, and an untrusted network, such as the Internet. This is known as a network, or perimeter, firewall. The other kind of firewall creates a barrier between a single computer, such as a laptop or desktop computer, and untrusted networks. This is known as a host-based firewall. Both firewalls examine incoming packets of data to see where they came from, how they were addressed, and what kind of data they might contain. For example, firewall software is designed to detect packets of data that contain malicious software, or malware for short, that is harmful to the operation of a computer. Hackers often use malware to penetrate firewalls and then perform certain tasks, such as copying computer files and sending them back to the hacker. Hackers are constantly disguising their malware in new ways, so firewall software must be continually updated with information about the new malware to prevent it from crossing through the barrier.

> **WORDS IN CONTEXT**
>
> **packet**
>
> a small unit of data that is routed from an origin to a destination and includes a delivery address and user information

User Account Access Controls ■

While firewalls are designed to keep intruders out, they also must allow authorized users in. Private networks and most computers give authorized users access to the network or device by having them verify their identity. This is done through a software program known as a user account access control. Most often the user account access control requires the user to know a combination of a user name and a password. Some types of access control require a person to use a secret user name as well as a secret password. However, on many networks—such as Gmail, Yahoo! Mail, and Windows Live—the user name is simply the user's e-mail address. For such accounts, all the hacker needs to know or discover is the user's password.

Most user account access control systems allow the user to create his or her own password. This is known as a user-defined password. Cybersecurity experts advise users to use a random series of letters, numbers, and even symbols rather than using a word or phrase. Using random characters makes it more difficult for hackers to guess the passwords or to discover them. Hackers can discover passwords by using a computer to try every possible combination of words and numbers—a technique known as a brute force attack. Users are encouraged not to use words that might be guessed, such as their own name, their spouse's name, a pet's name, their street address, or anything else a hacker might be able to guess with a little information about the person.

The software for some user account access control systems automatically rejects easily guessable passwords. The software measures password strength and will not accept a user-defined password until it meets a minimum level of complexity. The password software often prompts the person creating the password to use a combination of both letters and numbers, and sometimes letters, numbers, and symbols.

Token-Defined Passwords ■

Passwords are so important to cybersecurity that some organizations go even further to ensure that their employees are using only strong passwords to gain entry to their networks. Instead of allowing the user to define the password, some user account access control systems require a person to provide a password generated by another device, such as a token.

Digital security provider RSA produces small, plastic tokens that can be attached to a keychain. The token has a built-in clock and is loaded with software that generates a six-digit passcode at fixed intervals—often every sixty seconds. The codes are generated by a unique encryption key, known as a seed, embedded in each device. When the user wants to log in to an account, he or she first enters a personal identification number, or PIN. That number tells the user account access control system which token is being used. The user then presses a button next to a small, monochromatic screen on the face of the token. The screen displays the six-digit number generated for that particular time, using the embedded seed. The token displays the number for a few seconds—just long enough for the user to type the passcode into the password field. The user account access control system

Some user account control systems now require the use of a token such as the one pictured as a security measure. The token generates a one-time password that is usable for only a few seconds.

checks that number against the number that the user's key should have generated at that time. If the two numbers match, the user gains access to the account. If not, the log-in fails. The next time the user needs to access the account, he or she repeats the process, and the token generates a new passcode. If the user (or a hacker) tries to use the same passcode at a different time, it will not work, because it is no longer valid.

The PIN that is paired with the token-defined password is often several digits long. For example, the Cisco AnyConnect network system requires the user to enter an eight-digit PIN followed by the six-digit token-defined password. This results in a fourteen-digit password that is only valid for a short period of time. Such a long password is nearly impossible to guess, and it is extremely difficult to discover, even with a brute force attack. For even greater security against brute force attacks, however, most user account access control systems lock the user out of the account after a small number of incorrect passwords have been tried.

Password Managers ■

Knowing that people find it hard to create, memorize, and securely store strong passwords, several software companies have developed programs known as password managers. These programs store and even create strong passwords. Once the user has entered all his or her user names and passwords into the password manager, he or she no longer needs to remember or keep a list of the information. When a user wants to access a website associated with a particular user name and password, the password manager automatically fills in the necessary information. Because the user does not type anything, no one can steal the password by watching the user type or by capturing the user's keystrokes using malware. In addition, the software automatically encrypts the passwords when storing them, preventing hackers from reading them.

The encryption feature requires the user to create one master password or multiple-word passphrase. In an ideal situation, the master passphrase is long, complicated, and includes letters, numbers, and symbols. The user must take extreme caution not to lose the master passphrase or leave it on any device where a hacker might find it.

Once a password manager is installed, the user can create extremely strong passwords for any new accounts without bothering to memorize or store them. The software does it automatically. In fact, the software even offers to create high-strength, randomly generated passwords for the user. Discussing a password manager called Dashlane, David Pogue of the *New York Times* writes, "Since Dashlane is now storing and auto-entering your passwords, you're now free to follow the security experts' advice. You can make up long, unguessable passwords—a different one for every Web site, since you don't have to remember any of them."[7]

In addition to passwords, password managers can store and encrypt personal information needed for online transactions, such as name, address, phone number, and credit card infor-

Bad Password Advice Brings Down a Presidential Candidate

According to an article in the *Atlantic*, John Podesta, the head of Hillary Clinton's presidential campaign, succumbed to a phishing scam, leading to the release of damaging campaign e-mails. The article states that Podesta received an e-mail disguised as an alert from Google, informing him that someone had tried to sign in to his Gmail account and advising him to change his password. An aide to Podesta forwarded the e-mail to the campaign's information technology help desk. The help desk staffer, Charles Delavan, wrote back, "This is a legitimate email. John needs to change his password immediately, and ensure that two-factor authentication is turned on [for] his account. It is absolutely imperative that this is done ASAP." Delavan later said he meant to type that the e-mail was "illegitimate," not "legitimate." The staffer sent Podesta a link to the authentic Google website where users can change their passwords, but Delavan's typographical error led Podesta to click the link in the phishing e-mail instead. He entered his current password as instructed and then created a new one, giving the hackers his actual password. They used the password to access Podesta's account and copy thousands of campaign e-mails. Many experts believe that the release of those e-mails hurt the credibility of presidential candidate Hillary Clinton and contributed to her narrow defeat in the 2016 presidential election.

Quoted in Kaveh Waddell, "Why Some People Think a Typo Cost Clinton the Election," *Atlantic*, December 16, 2016. www.theatlantic.com.

mation, including the card number, the expiration date, and the security code printed on the back of the card. When performing an online transaction, the user simply selects a picture of the payment method he or she wants to use (so there are no keystrokes for hackers to intercept), and the password manager places the data in the correct boxes. "Every time you order something online, you save between 30 seconds and five minutes, depending on whether you have your card information memorized or have to go burrow through your wallet,"[8] writes Pogue.

Log-In Alerts ■

Passwords are such a vital part of cybersecurity that many online companies automatically send users a text message, e-mail, or smartphone alert, known as a push notification, whenever their passwords change. The alert may require the user to confirm that he or she, not a hacker, changed the password. Some financial institutions and credit card companies also send alerts whenever customers conduct an online transaction. Dan Kaminsky believes such notifications must be part of a person's own cybersecurity defense. "If you have a bank account that will not send you a text message when there's a transaction, move your money," advises Kaminsky. "Because now it's not about preventing the fraud, it's about seeing it as soon as it happens."[9]

Hacking has become so commonplace that some companies even send alerts whenever a user logs in to an account from a new device or from an unusual physical location. If the user did

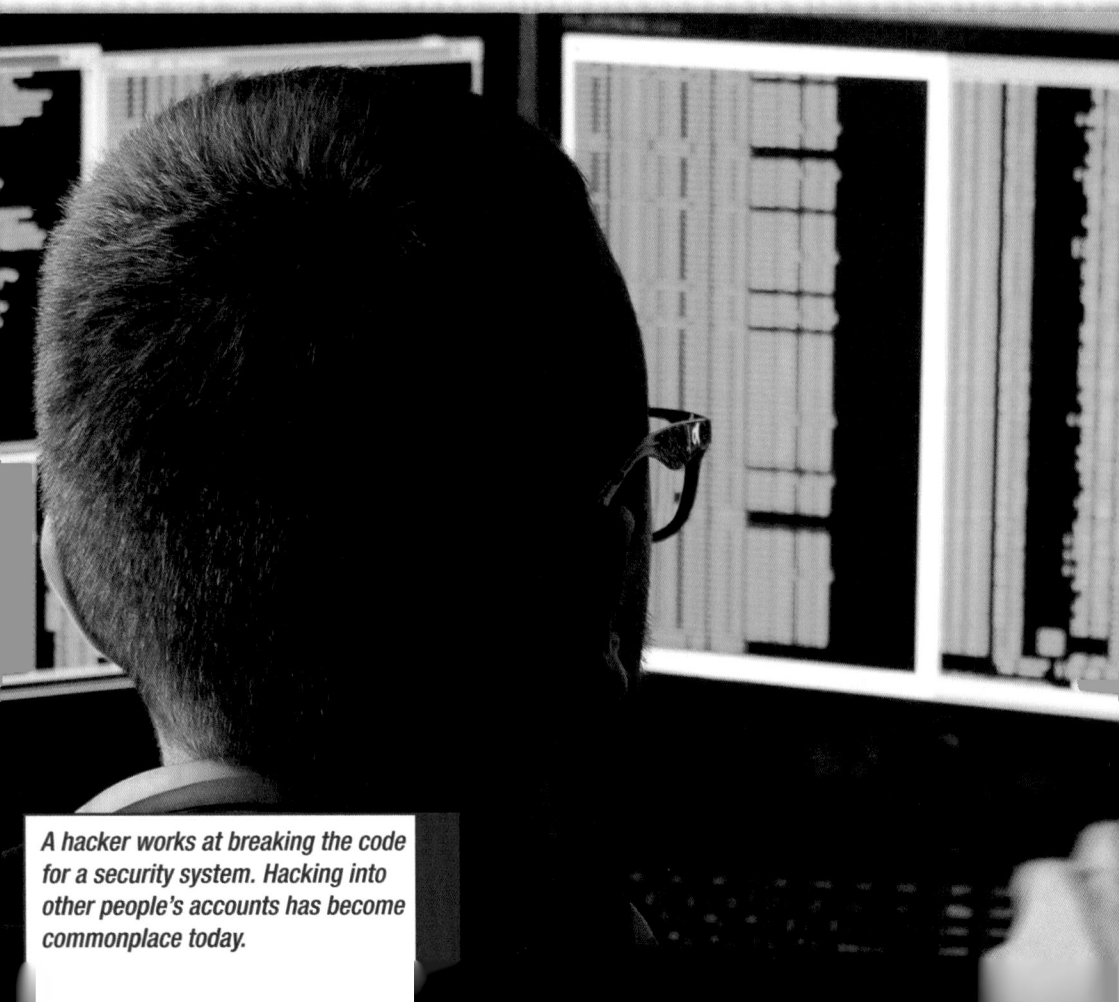

A hacker works at breaking the code for a security system. Hacking into other people's accounts has become commonplace today.

not use a new device or log in from a new location, the alert advises him or her to immediately log in to the account and change the password. These steps may inconvenience the user, but they also help defeat hackers.

Host Intrusion Detection Systems ■

Some hackers are able to slip past user account access controls and gain unauthorized access to systems residing behind the firewall, but that does not mean that cybersecurity has been defeated. Further measures often are in place to stop the hackers or their malware even after access to the system has been gained. One such security measure is known as a host intrusion detection (HID) system. This is a type of software that monitors activity within the host—a network, software program, database, or individual computer—watching for unusual activity that would be a sign of an intruder, such as a malware program or a hacker. Creators of this kind of software assume that hackers are not interested in just looking around a system. Rather, they want to take some action, such as stealing valuable data like customer records, or cause some damage, like deleting files or encrypting data so the user has to pay a ransom to access it.

A HID system uses automation to detect intrusions and alert a security expert when it finds that something unusual is happening. Sometimes the automated system will take more drastic action, such as shutting down the area where the intrusion has been detected. For example, if the system detects a large number of files being accessed, copied, or deleted, it might shut down the affected computer. Since most organizations keep backups of their data, any files deleted by a hacker or malware can usually be restored. In this way the HID system can limit the size and scope of the damage. Similarly, the system might detect a large amount of data being moved from one part of the system to another or exported through the firewall. Again, the intrusion detection software might halt the activity until a security expert can determine whether the action is authorized.

Antivirus Software ■

Malware is one of the most difficult hacking tools to stop from passing through a firewall. These small, automated programs can be

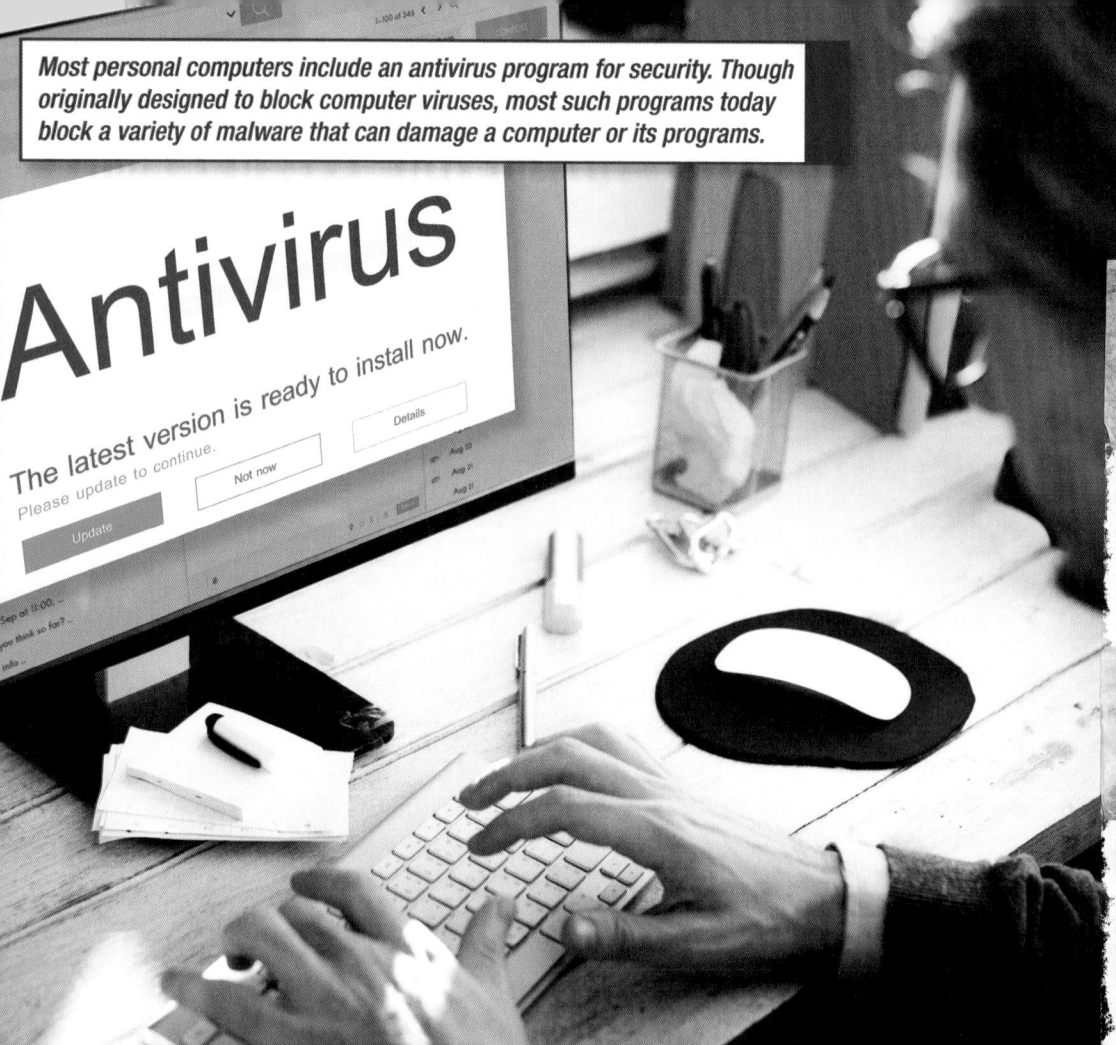

hidden within larger files, such as e-mails and e-mail attachments. Malware also can be downloaded from websites without the Internet user knowing it is happening. Once inside a computer, the malware can begin to work, or execute, as soon as the user opens or even previews the file to which the malware is attached. To prevent such programs from damaging computers, databases, or networks, security experts have designed software to detect and stop malware. This software was first developed to detect malware known as viruses, and it is still known as antivirus software. However, modern antivirus software can now detect a wide range of malware. This can include adware, a program that presents unwanted advertisements to the user; spyware, which monitors user activity and sends information back to the program creator; browser hijackers, which open unwanted web pages and do not allow the browser to close them; and Trojan horses, malicious programs disguised as something helpful. Malware also includes ransomware, which locks a user out of the computer until he or she pays money, a ransom, to unlock the computer. Malware also includes self-replicating programs known as worms.

Most antivirus software uses two approaches to detect malware. The most common method is for the antivirus software to scan the strings of binary numbers that make up the software code on the user's computer. The antivirus software then compares these strings of numbers to the strings of numbers known to be used in malware. This type of scanning is similar to the process the firewall uses to try to prevent malware from entering the computer in the first place. When the antivirus software finds a match between a string of numbers in the code on a computer and a string of numbers in known malware, it will automatically stop the program from running and disable the malware. The "infected" files are isolated on the computer's hard disk and prevented from infecting other files. This process is known as quarantining.

Heuristic Analysis ■

The second most common method of malware detection is known as heuristic analysis, or sandboxing. This process is similar to HID systems because it monitors the activity of a software program to see whether any of it looks suspicious. However, unlike HID systems, heuristic analysis is performed within an area separated from the rest of the computer's operating system, sometimes referred to as a sandbox. The heuristic analysis software allows the suspicious program to open in this isolated environment to see how it behaves. If the program does what it is designed to do, the heuristic analysis software leaves it intact. However, if it begins to overwrite files, make copies of itself, or take other malicious actions, the heuristic analysis software flags the program as potential malware and alerts the user. Because the malicious activity occurs only within a simulated environment, the real-world computer is not harmed by the malware.

Ransomware

A form of malware known as ransomware has become the most common and expensive form of hacking. According to research firm Malwarebytes, ransomware accounted for 60 percent of all malware infections in 2016. Network security firm SonicWall reports that businesses experienced 638 million ransomware attacks in 2016 and paid out more than $1 billion to hackers.

In a typical ransomware attack, the malware encrypts computer files so they cannot be read without a decrypting device, known as a key. The malware launches a screen that states "Your personal files are encrypted." The hackers demand money, or ransom, for the decryption key. The screen warns, "Any attempt to remove or damage this software will lead to the immediate destruction of the private key by the server." To pay the hackers, the user clicks a link and authorizes payment to the hacker's account. "Over the last few years attackers realized that instead of going through these elaborate hacks—phishing for passwords, breaking into accounts, stealing information, and then selling the data on the internet's black market for pennies per record—they could simply target individuals and businesses and treat them like an ATM," says Brian Beyer, chief executive officer of security firm Red Canary.

Quoted in Dan Tynan, "The State of Cyber Security: We're All Screwed," *Guardian* (Manchester), August 8, 2016. www.theguardian.com.

Because heuristic analysis monitors activity, rather than simply comparing a computer's code strings to the code strings of known malware, it sometimes discovers previously unknown malware or variations of known malware. After such a discovery is made, the heuristic analysis software sends a report back to the antivirus company, informing it of the new, malicious code. The software can also send the company a copy of suspicious code for further testing. If the new code is confirmed as malware, the antivirus software provider can add it to the list of known malware so firewalls and intrusion detection systems will recognize it.

Firewalls, HID systems, and antivirus software are not perfect. Hackers can overcome any one of them. However, when they are used together, they can prevent many cyberattacks and keep successful attacks from doing extensive damage to computer systems. "Integrated security tools working together in an automated architecture can streamline the process of detecting and mitigating threats," states computer technology corporation Cisco in its *2017 Annual Cybersecurity Report*. Most organizations use several security products at the same time to prevent or quickly discover hacking. "A majority of companies use more than five security vendors and more than five security products in their environment," reports Cisco. "Fifty-five percent of security professionals use at least six vendors."[10]

Designing an effective cybersecurity system using cutting edge security products is an important and rewarding profession. Cybersecurity experts know they are preventing hackers from doing harm to individuals, companies, and even their nation. "For top talent, cybersecurity isn't about just a job and a paycheck," says Jim Duffey, secretary of technology at the office of the governor of Virginia. "It is about the hottest technology, deployed by honorable organizations, for a purpose that is inherently important."[11]

CHAPTER 2

PROBLEMS: Weaknesses Exploited by Hackers

"The biggest threat to security isn't increasingly sophisticated cyber criminals, data-hungry corporations or even espionage-happy nation states; it's the people who get duped into clicking random links or opening rogue files. To paraphrase Pogo: we have met the cyber enemy, and he is us."

—Dan Tynan, technology journalist

Dan Tynan, "The State of Cyber Security: We're All Screwed," *Guardian* (Manchester), August 8, 2016. www .theguardian.com.

In 1987 Frederick B. Cohen, a computer scientist who created one of the first computer viruses, showed that no antivirus program can perfectly detect all possible viruses. He based his conclusion on the principle of undecidability; that is, the idea that antivirus software can never determine for certain whether a program is harmful until it begins to work. As a result, antivirus programs only make educated guesses about programs, based on statistics and probability. So far, Cohen has been proved right. According to the Identity Theft Resource Center, in 2016 (the last year for which statistics are available) US companies and government agencies suffered a record 1,093 data breaches. This was a 40 percent increase from 2015. Clearly, hackers are taking advantage of a wide range of cybersecurity weaknesses.

Password Weaknesses ■

User-defined passwords are the keys that unlock most smartphones, computers, networks, and accounts, and many users take them seriously. However, many do not. They use the shortest possible password and often use all letters or all numbers, rather than mixing them up. This makes it easier for hackers to guess a password or to steal it using brute force. Many users also create passwords related to their personal lives, using things such as their street address, spouse's name, or the name of a school they attended. Hackers often use information gathered from online profiles to guess such simple passwords. Even worse, some users never change the password that was originally set up on the computer, known as the default password. Common default passwords include "password," "admin," or "1234." Using a default password is like locking the door to your house and leaving the key under the mat, where anyone who looks can find it. According to Verizon's *2016 Data Breach Investigations Report*, "63 percent of confirmed data breaches leverage a weak, default, or stolen password."[12]

For simplicity's sake, many people use the same password for all of their accounts. This is one reason the Yahoo! and Myspace hacks—which together affected more than 1 billion users—were important. The hackers might not have cared about getting into those accounts, but they realized that a number of people will use the same user name and password for many other accounts, including online banking and retail accounts. Research suggests that gaining the passwords people use for their free e-mail accounts and online cloud storage can be more profitable for hackers than attacking financial institutions directly. In February 2017 cybersecurity firm Webroot reported:

> WORDS IN CONTEXT
>
> **phishing**
>
> attempting to obtain private information such as user names, passwords, and credit card details for malicious reasons by pretending to be a trustworthy entity in an electronic communication

The 2017 Webroot Threat Report today revealed that for every new phishing URL impersonating a financial institution, there were more than seven impersonating technology companies. The data was collected throughout 2016 by Webroot . . . and clearly demonstrates a significant change since 2015, when the ratio was less than one to three. This increase may indicate that it is easier to phish a technology account, and that due to password reuse, they can be more valuable to hackers as a gateway to other accounts. The top three phishing targets in 2016 were Google, Yahoo and Apple.[13]

Internet service provider Yahoo! in late 2016 announced that its servers had been breached by hackers twice. Affecting more than 1.5 billion accounts, the breaches are two of the largest in Internet history.

Once inside an e-mail account, hackers can search to see where the user does business, and then try the same user name and password to gain access to a more fruitful account, such as an online bank account. Most hackers do not do this manually; they use software programs to automatically look for user name and password matches on a wide range of targeted websites.

One of the remedies for weak passwords is software known as password strength programs. These programs require users to create complex passwords using words, numbers, and symbols. If a password is not complex enough, the software will not allow the user to employ it. Users must continue adding characters until they create a password of acceptable strength.

Password strength programs eliminate weak user-defined passwords, but they can also produce weaknesses of their own. Sometimes the resulting password is so complex that the user will jot the password down on a piece of paper or save it in a text file, out of fear of forgetting it. Both of these actions create security risks because anyone who finds the paper or accesses the text file can learn the password and use it to gain access to accounts. In addition, some Internet browsers, such as Google Chrome, offer to save a password every time the user creates a new one. If the user allows the browser to remember the password, the browser will automatically fill in the password the next time the user visits the website requiring it. This feature is convenient for the user, especially when the password is difficult to remember. However, it also is risky, because whoever has access to the computer can use the automatic password feature to gain access to accounts. The intruder can then change the passwords and use the new ones to access the account from another computer.

Exploiting Systems ■

Sometimes hackers can penetrate a system even without knowing any passwords. For example, they might find an older device connected to a network with an easily exploited operating system or one that has not been updated with security patches that can identify new malware.

In 2016 the cybersecurity firm TrapX Security investigated ten cases in which hackers penetrated hospital computer networks through unsecured medical devices such as X-ray machines, blood gas analyzers, and magnetic resonance imaging machines. Computers in these devices allow medical technicians to run tests on patients and send the results to the hospital computer network. But the computers in such devices lack the processing power to run sophisticated security software. "The standard cyber security environment set up in the hospital, regardless of how effective it might be, cannot access the internal software operations of medical devices,"[14] explains Carl Wright, executive vice president and general manager of TrapX Security. For privacy reasons, TrapX did not identify which hospitals were targeted or which malware was used, but once inside the

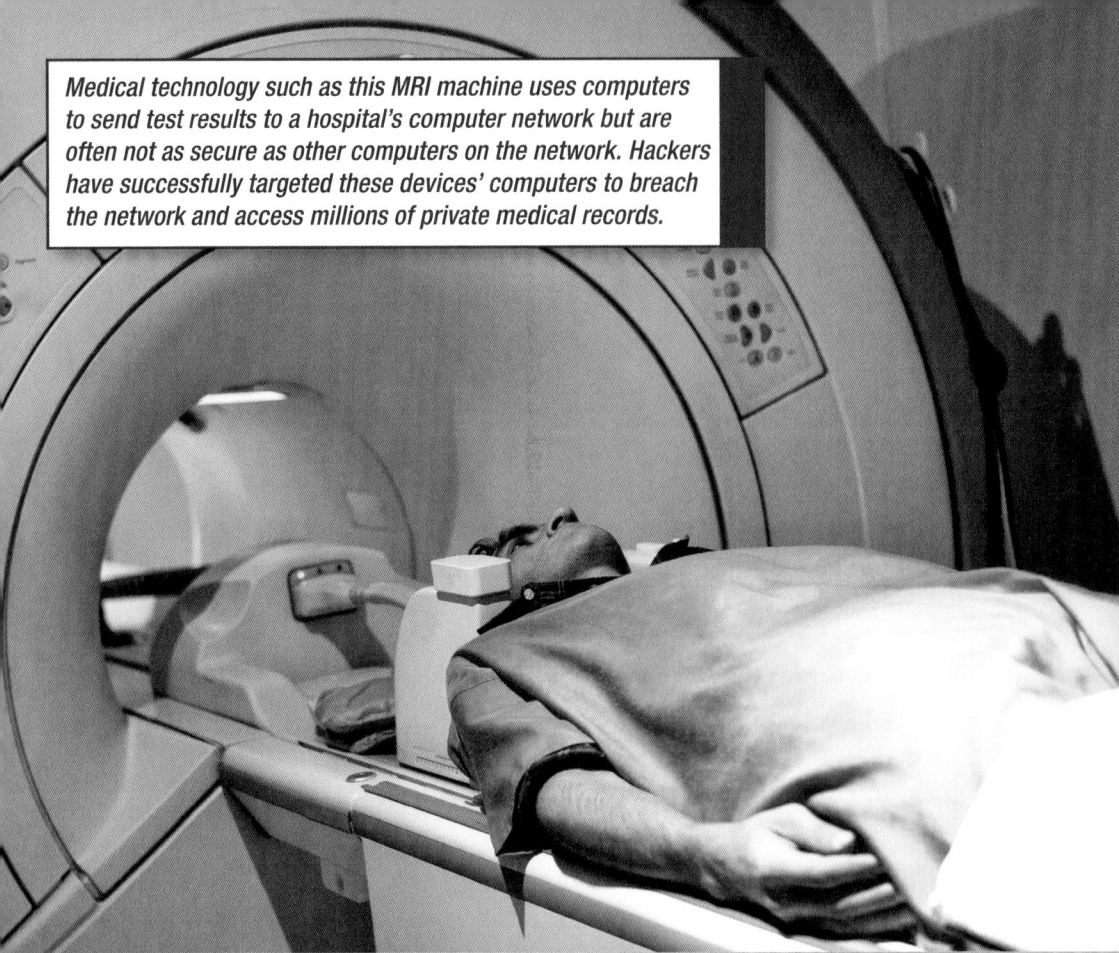

Medical technology such as this MRI machine uses computers to send test results to a hospital's computer network but are often not as secure as other computers on the network. Hackers have successfully targeted these devices' computers to breach the network and access millions of private medical records.

hospital computer networks, the malware sent passwords and other information back to the hackers. This allowed the hackers to set up a "back door" into the system so they could access hospital records. "The records enable fraudulent access to the victim's financial accounts including bank accounts, credit card accounts and more," says Moshe Ben-Simon, cofounder and vice president of TrapX Security. "Medical records are the top targets for cyber attackers."[15]

Expanding the Attack Surface ■

Hospitals are not the only places where networked devices offer hackers relatively easy access to computer systems. The number of small, difficult-to-secure devices is growing exponentially in businesses and homes alike. This network of devices is known as the Internet of Everything (IoE). It includes "smart" home electronic devices, such as televisions, home alarm systems, air-conditioning controls, even refrigerators and exercise equipment. According to the market research firm Gartner, 5.5 million new devices are connecting to the IoE every day. The research firm estimated that 6.4 billion devices would be connected to the IoE by the end of 2016, a number that will grow to nearly 21 billion by 2020. Such devices send digital data over wireless networks to smartphones and computers, which in turn are further linked to bank accounts and other vital information. Since the devices are small, they have limited security capabilities, and hackers can exploit them to gain access to wider systems.

Cybersecurity experts refer to the sudden adoption of such devices as an expansion of the attack surface. "The proliferation of mobile devices creates more endpoints to protect," states the *Cisco 2017 Annual Cybersecurity Report*. "As businesses embrace digitization—and the Internet of Everything (IoE) begins to take shape—defenders will have even more to worry about. The attack surface will only expand, giving adversaries more space to operate."[16]

Low-Tech Attacks ■

Cybersecurity is a high-tech field that uses some of the most advanced computer technology in existence, but sometimes it can be defeated by the simplest low-tech techniques. For example, hackers successfully penetrated the highly secure computer network of Iran's Natanz nuclear centrifuge facility simply by loading malware onto portable data storage devices, known as flash drives or memory sticks, that plug in to a computer's USB port and then leaving the devices in locations inside or near the facility. At some point a Natanz employee picked up one of the flash drives and inserted it into a USB port on a company network computer, just to see what was on it. The malware, known as the Stuxnet worm, entered the computer, replicated itself, and traveled through the network, infecting other computers. Eventually, the malware traveled to a computer that controlled the centrifuges that were used to purify, or enrich, nuclear material. Finding the type of software it was programmed to look for, the Stuxnet worm took control of the centrifuges and made them spin at a higher rate than they were designed to withstand, which caused the machines to tear themselves apart. Intelligence experts believe that hackers destroyed one-fifth of Iran's nuclear centrifuges, slowing the country's progress toward developing a nuclear bomb.

The Natanz employee was not the only person to succumb to curiosity and connect a found flash drive to a computer. Indeed, hackers use this technique because it works. In a 2015 study, a team of researchers at the University of Illinois, Urbana-Champaign, found that 45 percent of the people who found flash drives that the researchers had planted around campus not only plugged the devices in to their computers but also proceeded to open files stored on the flash drive. "It's easy to laugh at these attacks, but the scary thing is that they work—and that's something that needs to be addressed,"[17] says Matthew Tischer, lead researcher of the study. About half of those who used the flash drives agreed to participate in an anonymous online survey about the project. Sixty-eight percent of those who responded to the survey told the researchers that they took no precautions when connecting the flash drive. Of those respondents who took protective measures, 16 percent scanned the drive with their antivirus software, and 8 percent believed their operating system or antivirus software would protect them. "I trust my macbook to be a good defense against viruses," one respondent told the researchers. As the researchers note, "In this paper, we showed that the anecdote that users will pick up and plug in flash drives they find is true. . . . In a controlled experiment at the University of Illinois, we find that the attack [was] both effective with an estimated 45% to 98% of dropped drives connected and expeditious with the first drive connected in under six minutes."[18]

Social Engineering Attacks ■

Hackers who take advantage of human traits such as curiosity to gain entry into computer systems are said to practice social engineering attacks. This can take many forms but usually involves tricking a computer user into providing access to an online account, computer, or network. A common social engineering attack is known as phishing. With this technique, the hacker sends an official-looking e-mail to a large number of people, hoping to persuade some of them to reveal their passwords or click on an attachment or a link that launches malware into their computer. The e-mail persuades people to surrender their passwords to attain some benefit, such as, ironically, protecting their account from a hack-

Health App Leaks Personal Information

As the Internet of Everything grows, millions of people are putting personal information on devices with limited cybersecurity protection. In 2016, Consumer Reports, a nonprofit organization that provides information about products, found that Glow, a smartphone app that helps women track their fertility, had a security flaw that would allow strangers to access a user's personal information. "Consumer Reports discovered that anyone who knew a user's email address could start getting that data without the user's explicit permission," wrote Andrea Peterson, a reporter for the *Washington Post*. "That means practically anyone, including stalkers or abusive exes, could have found a window into the intimate data the app tracked." The information includes details not only about the user's menstrual cycle, but also about her alcohol consumption and sexual activity. "This kind of information for women is very intimate," said Deborah Peel, a privacy rights activist. "The implications are really huge: There are absolutely no laws that protect that information from being sold, disclosed, or traded—for any purpose, be it marketing or research." Glow, which claims to have helped 150,000 couples conceive, said it had no evidence that any personal data had been accessed by unauthorized users before it fixed the security problem.

Quoted in Andrea Peterson, "Watch Out, Ladies: Your Period-Tracking App Could Be Leaking Personal Data," *Washington Post*, August 3, 2016. www.washingtonpost.com.

ing attempt. According to a 2015 study by Verizon that combined the results of 8 million phishing tests conducted by various security companies, "30% of phishing messages were opened by the target across all campaigns. About 12% went on to click the malicious attachment or link and thus enabled the attack to succeed."[19]

Phishing succeeds because it is easier to fool people than it is to breach firewalls or defeat antivirus programs. "Users are, and always will be, a weak link in the security chain,"[20] states the *Cisco 2017 Annual Cybersecurity Report*. According to Verizon, 91 percent of all successful security breaches are launched via phishing scams. The cybersecurity firm Wombat Security Technologies reports that 76 percent of US companies reported that their organizations were victims of a phishing attack in 2016.

Hackers Take Control of a Baby Monitor

Hackers are exploiting security weaknesses in the Internet of Everything to invade home computer networks. In 2015 a woman in Whitewater, Kansas, noticed that the camera of her wireless baby monitor was following her as she moved around in her child's room. "Every single hair on my body stood up," the woman told a local television station. "I was freaked out . . . like very, very scary actually." When she left the room to see if the handheld viewing device was malfunctioning, the camera followed her. "I knew someone was watching me. I yelled into the camera and I was like, 'quit watching me' but I didn't know what to do. I was just so scared and so shocked that this is actually happening to me."

The woman had put a password on the baby monitor, but because she lived in a rural area, she did not put one on her wireless modem. The hackers were therefore able to gain control of the baby monitor through the modem. "I want all the moms out there to know that you're not technically safe just because you either live in the country or you don't have any neighbors," said the woman. "I want them to know to put passwords on these things and monitor whether someone is accessing them or not."

Quoted in Darlene Storm, "2 More Wireless Baby Monitors Hacked: Hackers Remotely Spied on Babies and Parents," *Computerworld*, April 22, 2015. www.computerworld.com.

The vast majority of phishing scams occur via e-mail, but an increasing number are occurring through social media. Cybersecurity provider Proofpoint reported that social media phishing attacks increased by 500 percent in the last three months of 2016 alone. In such attacks, users of social media such as Facebook or Twitter are typically asked to click on a link that takes them to a website, where they are asked to provide information that hackers can then exploit. The phishing websites exist only to collect information, and they are not online for long. "The longest-running phishing site was active less than two days, and the shortest was only 15 minutes," stated Webroot in its annual security report. "Eighty-four percent of all phishing sites were active for less than 24 hours."[21] The short lifetime of phishing websites makes it difficult to catch the hackers behind them.

Physical Intrusion ■

Most hackers hide behind websites and e-mails, but some actually come face-to-face with their intended victims. According to *The State of Cybersecurity and Digital Trust 2016* report by HfS Research and Accenture, 69 percent of the organizations surveyed had experienced attempted or successful data theft or corruption by people actually working at the organizations during the previous twelve months. The rate was even higher in media and technology companies, with 77 percent of the organizations reporting data attacks by corporate insiders.

Sometimes physical intrusion is not done by authorized employees but by hackers in disguise. Some gain entrance to a facility by pretending to be maintenance workers, cleaning crews, or computer technicians. Once inside, the hackers attempt to hack into the system at an unattended workstation or to load a flash drive containing malware into an open computer. According to the HfS Research and Accenture cybersecurity report, the threat posed by employees and nonemployees who gain access to offices is so great that many security professionals are making physical security a high priority. *The State of Cybersecurity and Digital Trust 2016* states:

> One positive data point from our research is the convergence of digital and physical security, with more than 30 percent of respondents rating unauthorized physical access in data and office facilities either a strong or critical concern. This level of attention can be viewed as positive in that it highlights an increased awareness of the importance of bringing physical and digital security together under a larger risk umbrella.[22]

The ultimate physical intrusion is the theft of a device—a laptop computer, smartphone, tablet, or a memory device such as an external hard drive or flash drive. Once the hacker possesses such a device, he or she has ample time and multiple ways to gain access to the data inside. The stored data can include an organization's secrets stored on the device or passwords that can be used in future hacks. Such devices can be stolen by intruders within a facility, but they can also be taken by thieves who follow a targeted person and then steal the device at a restaurant, coffee shop, or airport. In a stunning breach of physical security, Harold Martin, a security contractor who worked at the National Security Agency (NSA), an intelligence organization of the federal government, stole hundreds of thousands of documents, most of them classified, over a twenty-year period. Martin did not hack into the NSA computers. He simply walked out of the building with hard drives, storage disks, and flash drives loaded with classified documents. "The security folks there conduct random bag and purse checks on people leaving, but nobody does pocket checks," a former employee who worked at the NSA for thirty years told ZDNet, a technology website. "Anything that could fit in a pocket could go out undetected,"[23] the employee said.

Phonies on the Phone ■

Another social engineering technique is to obtain passwords or other information hackers could use, such as bank card numbers or Social Security numbers, through a phone call, sometimes referred to as voice phishing, or "vishing." During tax season in 2017, a large number of tax preparers were successfully targeted by scammers impersonating representatives from companies that provide electronic tax return software. The hackers claimed that the tax preparers' software was corrupted or out of date and then requested remote access to their computers. Once permission was granted and the remote access software was installed, the hackers could control the users' computers. The hackers promised to fix or update the software, but they actually used the remote access to take over the tax professionals' accounts and steal information such as their clients' tax returns, bank information, and credit card numbers.

Tax professionals are hardly alone in being targeted by vishing scams. Businesses and individuals alike receive phone calls from scammers pretending to represent trusted companies, such as a phone company or Internet provider, or government agencies, such as law enforcement or the IRS. According to the

> ## WORDS IN CONTEXT
>
> ### vishing
>
> a term blending *voice* and *phishing*, used to describe a scam conducted by telephone in which the scammer attempts to obtain sensitive information such as user names, passwords, and credit card details for malicious reasons

Hackers often gain access to people's private data by randomly phoning people and impersonating a bank or credit bureau official. The hacker persuades the target to divulge credit card or Social Security numbers over the phone, then uses that data to gain access to the target's private accounts.

inspector general of the US Department of the Treasury, more than four hundred thousand Americans received phone calls from scammers impersonating IRS officials in 2015. The majority of the scammers demanded that the victim send payment for tax bills, but a large number were vishing for Social Security numbers, bank account numbers, and credit card information. "The Treasury Inspector General for Tax Administration has called this scam 'the largest, most pervasive impersonation scam in the history of the IRS,'"[24] says Senator Susan Collins of Maine, who participated in a Senate hearing on the IRS impersonation scam.

From low-tech vishing scams to high-tech attacks on unsecured devices, hackers are seeking and getting access to digital information in ever-increasing numbers. According to Cisco, 44 percent of security operations managers see more than five thousand security alerts per day, but they are able to investigate only 56 percent of them. In addition, about 6.5 percent of all global e-mail is classified as malicious. Hackers seem to be getting the upper hand in the never-ending battle for online security. "Adversaries have more tools at their disposal than ever before," states the Cisco annual cybersecurity report. "They also have a keen sense of when to use each one for maximum effect. The explosive growth of mobile endpoints and online traffic works in their favor. They have more space in which to operate and more choices of targets and approaches."[25] The situation is bleak, but cybersecurity experts are not giving up. They are constantly devising new strategies and technologies to limit the number of successful attacks and to shorten the time hackers have to exploit a system.

WORDS IN CONTEXT

remote access

the ability to gain access to a computer or a computer network from a distant location via the Internet

CHAPTER 3

SOLUTIONS: Strengthening Personal Identification

"Relying on just a password today for securing an account . . . is no longer acceptable."

—Marc Boroditsky, vice president of Authy, a division of cloud-based communications provider Twilio

Quoted in Meg Bryant, "Pro Tips on Strengthening Cybersecurity," Healthcare Dive, August 11, 2016. www.healthcaredive.com.

The vast majority of hackers gain access to computer systems by outsmarting human computer users. This can involve defeating users' weak passwords, exploiting vulnerabilities created when users fail to keep their systems up-to-date, and stealing users' devices. As a result, cybersecurity engineers are always looking for ways to strengthen user account access control systems, motivate users to update their security systems, and track down or disable lost or stolen devices.

Overcoming Password Weakness ■

Whether hackers attempt to breach security by gaining access to an online account, an unattended workstation, or even a stolen device, they almost always need to defeat a user account access control system such as password protection. Using software that demands a certain level of password strength and requires users to include token-defined passwords are two methods that are being used to overcome password weakness, but engineers are designing new user account access control systems that will let users in and keep hackers out.

While the popularity of smartphones has expanded the cyberattack surface, it has also given cybersecurity engineers new pathways to securing devices and accounts. The most common of these is called two-factor authentication, also known as 2FA or TFA. The principle is simple: Hackers might be able to steal or guess a password, but they are far less likely to also have access to a second device belonging to the user. 2FA requires users to access a second device—often a smartphone—to verify their identity when they are logging in. A password by itself is not enough. By verifying that a user is physically present at log-in, the system prevents hacking from remote locations.

Most 2FA systems are used by organizations that want to increase the security of their networks or databases when employees and other users try to access them from a remote location—whether working from home or on the road thousands of miles away. The companies usually do not develop the 2FA

Two-factor authentication, or 2FA, systems help enhance online security. Such systems require a user logging into an account via a computer to provide identity authentication on another device, such as a smartphone, as well.

systems themselves. Instead, they purchase a system from companies that specialize in network, or enterprise, security. If the 2FA system requires the user to have a computer accessory to log in, the organization will supply the device to the employee, contractor, or vendor for free. 2FA systems used for online banking or other websites often employ the user's smartphone to authenticate. The company pays the 2FA supplier for the application, and the user simply downloads it for free. 2FA systems are available for home computers, too. Home users can either buy the software online and use it with a smartphone or buy the 2FA accessory and matching software at a local computer or electronics store.

Using a 2FA System ■

The most common form of 2FA requires the user to enter a temporary, unique passcode that is either generated using a special application installed on a smartphone, such as Google Authenticator, or sent as a text message to a regular cellular phone. The passcode only works for a certain amount of time, typically thirty to sixty seconds. After receiving the passcode, the user types it into a special field on the log-in page, thereby authenticating his or her identity and gaining access. Unless a hacker is in possession of the user's cell phone at the time of log-in, he or she will not be able to enter the passcode or gain access to the system or account.

Other 2FA systems use a callback method: The user receives a phone call at log-in and responds by pressing a key on the phone to authenticate. The user does not have to enter a complicated code; just being in possession of the registered cell phone is evidence of the user's identity. Some websites always ask for the 2FA, but others require it only when something appears suspicious, such as a log-in from a new Internet protocol (IP) address or an unusual physical location—a new city, state, or country.

An enhancement to 2FA that does not require users to enter a passcode is available to smartphone users from various companies. The user downloads a special 2FA mobile app. After logging in with a user name and password, the website will ask the user how he or she wishes to authenticate. If the user chooses "send me a push," the mobile app receives a message when the user is trying to access an online account and displays a push notification on the user's smartphone. The user taps the push notification, which opens the app. The user then has a choice to press buttons to accept or deny access. If the user is logging in, he or she simple presses "accept," and access is immediately granted. However, if the user is not logging in at the time he or she receives a push notification—if it is a hacker instead—the user can press "deny." This option prevents the hacker from gaining access to the account, and it also notifies the authentication provider of an unauthorized log-in attempt.

An alternative 2FA app uses Quick Response code (QR code) technology to verify the identity of the person logging in to a website via a computer. After entering a user name and password, the website displays a machine-readable matrix bar code—the black-and-white square bar code familiar to smartphone users. The user opens the authentication app and uses the smartphone camera to scan the QR code. Since the smartphone is registered to the user, the bar code scan will only authenticate the log-in if it comes from the user's phone. If a hacker with the same app on a different smartphone tries to scan the bar code, it will not grant access because that is not the smartphone registered to the user. In each form of 2FA, the user (or at least the user's cell phone or smartphone) must be present at the time of the log-in, verifying the user's identity.

Not all forms of 2FA use cell phones or smartphones. Others employ devices specifically designed for 2FA. These devices are often referred to as dongles. Dongles come in many forms, but all, like phones, verify the user's physical presence at the time of log-in. This ensures that the user's password is not being entered by a hacker.

Some dongles are flash drives loaded with numbers known as keys. When the user attempts to log in to a website, the website sends a challenge to the user's computer via its Internet browser, requesting a key. The user's dongle responds by sending a key back to the website, a process known as signing. If the key sent back to the website is one of the numbers assigned to the user, the log-in is completed. If not, the log-in is stopped. One advantage of

Empty-Handed Authentication

In an October 2016 blog post devoted to the future of cybersecurity, Jun Hosoi, a product manager for GlobalSign, a provider of identity verification systems, predicted that authentication will become much easier in the future:

> I believe "empty-handed" authentication will become the norm. Users won't need to have a smart card, a one-time password device, smartphone call back or a password and ID to log into devices and services.

> Instead, when users log into their PC, the camera on their PC will detect and identify they are the PC owner through facial recognition.

> And when someone buys something at a shop in their fitness club for example, or makes a withdrawal from their bank account, they will just need to put their finger on a scanner device. The device will read their finger vein pattern (or fingerprint) and identify them, then they can continue to access the service or purchase an item. . . .

> The idea is that we are moving into a future where we will not need to remember anything, or have anything in order to access services or purchase items. Soon we will be able to do everything "empty-handed."

Jun Hosoi, "The Future of Cybersecurity: Predictions from GlobalSign," *GlobalSign Blog*, GlobalSign, October 28, 2016. www.globalsign.com.

this system is that it does not require the user to press any keys, which could be intercepted by malware and given to a hacker—a method known as keystroke logging or key logging. Another advantage is that the dongle communicates directly with the website, bypassing any authentication providers that could be subject to "man-in-the-middle" attacks by hackers.

Biometric Identification ■

2FA using phones and dongles is designed to show that the account user is physically present at log-in. However, the device the user employs to complete the authentication could be stolen by a hacker. Since the device cannot verify the actual person using it, such authentication is not foolproof. Because of this, engineers have designed 2FA systems that use biological measurements, known as biometrics, to establish that the person logging in really is the owner of the device or account.

Fingerprints have been shown to be unique to every person, and they have been used for decades for identification in birth records, driver's licenses, passports, and other official documents. Some high-security buildings have electronic security systems that use fingerprint scanners to verify the identities of people before they are allowed to enter. Electronic fingerprint scanning is being incorporated into cybersecurity systems as well.

WORDS IN CONTEXT

biometric

relating to the analysis or measurement of unique physical characteristics used to identify individuals

Smartphones were among the first devices to use biometric technology to verify the identity of the user. Fingerprint scanning was first used on Toshiba smartphones in 2007. Apple introduced its fingerprint scanning system, Touch ID, on its iPhone 5S in 2013, and has been using it ever since. Many other smartphone makers have followed the trend. "Touch ID is a seamless way to use your fingerprint as a passcode," says Apple's website. "Your fingerprint is one of the best passcodes in the world. It's always with you, and no two are exactly alike. With just a touch of your device's Home button, the Touch ID sensor quickly reads your fingerprint and automatically unlocks your phone."[26]

How Fingerprint Scanners Work ■

Apple's fingerprint scanner uses a laser-cut sapphire crystal as a lens. Sapphire is extremely hard and not easily scratched—an important quality, since a scratched lens would prevent an accurate scan of the fingerprint. The lens is located inside a steel ring that acts as a sensor. The user does not press a button but instead simply places his or her finger over the ring, which initiates the scan. To establish the user's unique identity, the reader takes many high-resolution images of the ridges on the user's fingertip. "Touch ID . . . maps out individual details in the ridges that are smaller than the human eye can see and even inspects minor variations in ridge direction caused by pores and edge structures,"[27] according to Apple's website. The software does not store images of the fingerprint, but instead translates its key features into a mathematical representation. As a result, it is impossible for anyone who somehow gets the smartphone to obtain the user's fingerprint or even to reverse engineer it from the mathematical record. Apple says the chances of two people having the same mathematical representation are less than one in fifty thousand, or about five times less likely than guessing a four-digit passcode. The system allows only five unsuccessful fingerprint match attempts before requiring the user to enter a passcode to unlock the device.

Apple introduced its fingerprint scanner into several other of its devices, including tablets and laptop computers. Apple users can also employ the system to authorize online purchases from the iTunes Store, App Store, and iBooks Store. Both Apple Pay mobile payment systems and Samsung Pay use fingerprint readers to authorize payment at retail outlets. Many laptop computers also employ fingerprint identification technology. If a computer or other device does not have the technology built in, a user can purchase a fingerprint scanner as an accessory that plugs into a USB port, bringing biometric security to any device.

Not everyone is convinced that fingerprint scans are more secure than passwords. "A password is inherently private," says Alvaro Bedoya, a law professor at Georgetown University. "The whole point of a password is that you don't tell anyone about it. . . . [But] I know what your fingerprint looks like if we have a drink and you leave your fingerprints on the pint glass."[28] To prove the vulnerability of fingerprint identification systems, researchers from mobile security firm Vkansee successfully demonstrated how to break into Apple's Touch ID system at the 2016 Mobile World Congress, a mobile phone trade show, using a fingerprint impression in a small piece of Play-Doh modeling compound.

Iris Scanning ■

Fingerprints are not the only physical feature unique to every human being. The colored part of the eye, the iris, also varies from person to person, making it an ideal biometric marker. Iris scanners have been developed for all kinds of high-security systems. For example, several countries use iris scans to confirm the identities of airline passengers, and some banks use them instead of bank cards and personal identification numbers to allow customers access to automated teller machines. "Each person's iris patterns are unique and unchanging, making iris recognition the most accurate—and rapid—means of biometric identity authentication," says Charles Koo, president and chief executive officer of Iris ID, the company that made the iris scanners for Qatar National Bank in Qatar. "This non-contact and sanitary solution is ideal to enhance security throughout the financial industry."[29] Iris scanning is being adapted to cybersecurity systems as well.

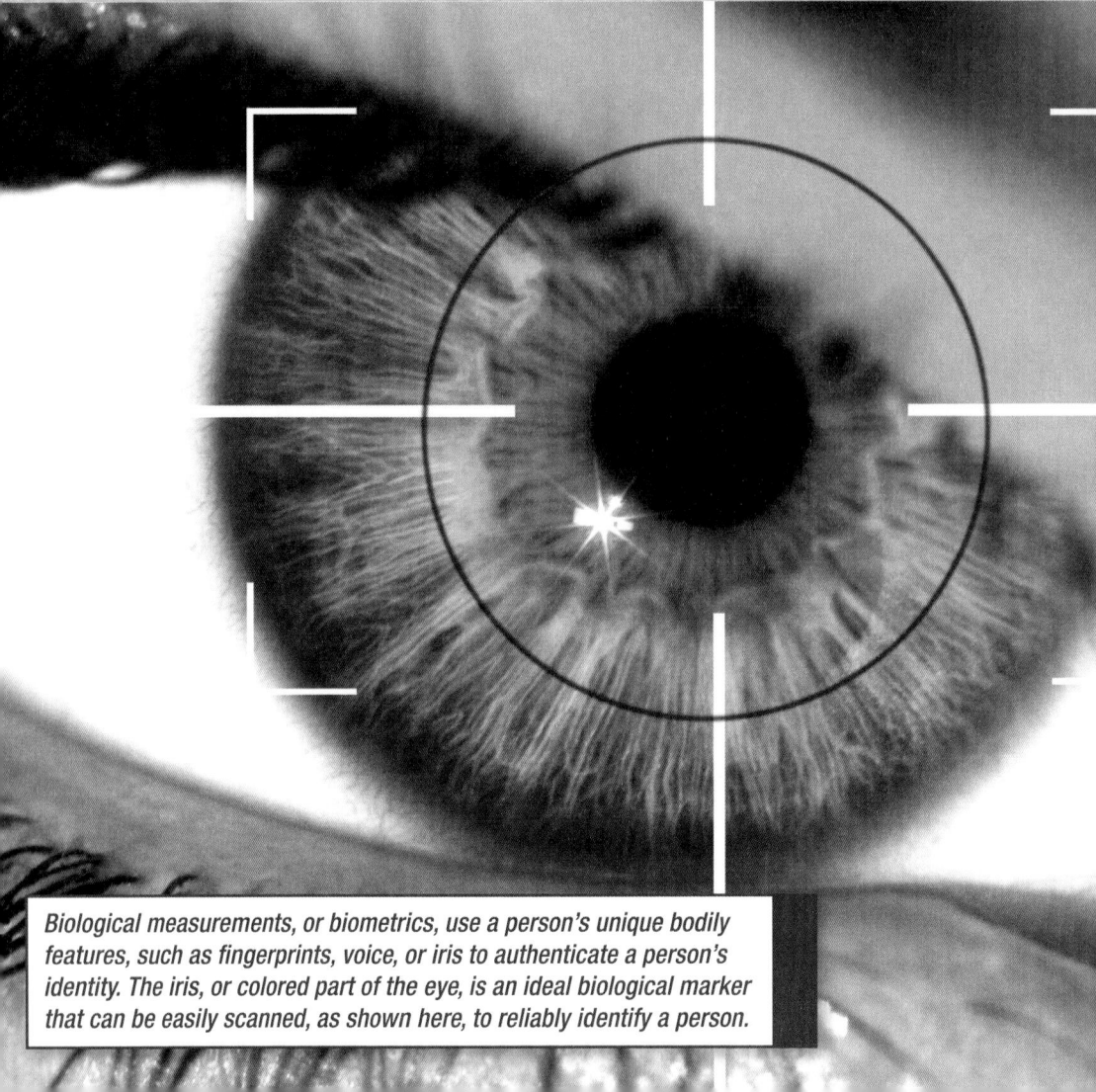

Biological measurements, or biometrics, use a person's unique bodily features, such as fingerprints, voice, or iris to authenticate a person's identity. The iris, or colored part of the eye, is an ideal biological marker that can be easily scanned, as shown here, to reliably identify a person.

Unlike fingerprints, which can be reconstructed from impressions left on various surfaces, the human iris is difficult to capture or reproduce. The scanner illuminates the iris with ordinary light and infrared light to bring out all the details of both light and dark eyes. The scanner takes a picture of the iris pattern and then records the positions of more than two hundred unique features and stores the numerical values in the device's memory. To verify identity, the user just looks into the camera and takes another picture. The device's software compares the image to the pattern stored in its memory. If the two match, the device will unlock. As with fingerprint technology, smartphones were the first to incorporate iris scanning into their security systems, but laptops also feature iris scanners as well.

Eye Vein Verification ■

Other phone makers have focused on another part of the eye that varies from person to person: the blood vessel pattern in the sclera, or the white part of the eye. Phone makers ViVo, ZTE, and Alcatel have teamed with up biometric scanner maker Eye-Verify to create systems that scan the whites of people's eyes to unlock phones—a system known as eye vein verification. To capture the images, the users must look first to one side and then to the other. The scanner captures an image each time, creating four distinct images—one from each side of each eye. As with fingerprint scanning, the images themselves are not stored, but they are mapped to create a mathematical record that is then compared to the eyes being scanned for identification. Unlike iris scanning, eye vein verification does not require a special light. The vein patterns are readily visible under normal lighting and can be scanned by most smartphone cameras, even through clear eyeglasses and with contact lenses in place. The blood vessel patterns do not change with age, and the accuracy of the scans are not affected by allergies, alcohol or drug consumption, or disease. As with iris scanning, the user does not come in contact with the scanner, so the process is more sanitary than fingerprint scanning.

Some biometric systems scan the entire face to confirm the identity of the user, a system known as facial recognition. Facial recognition software identifies dozens of unique characteristics of

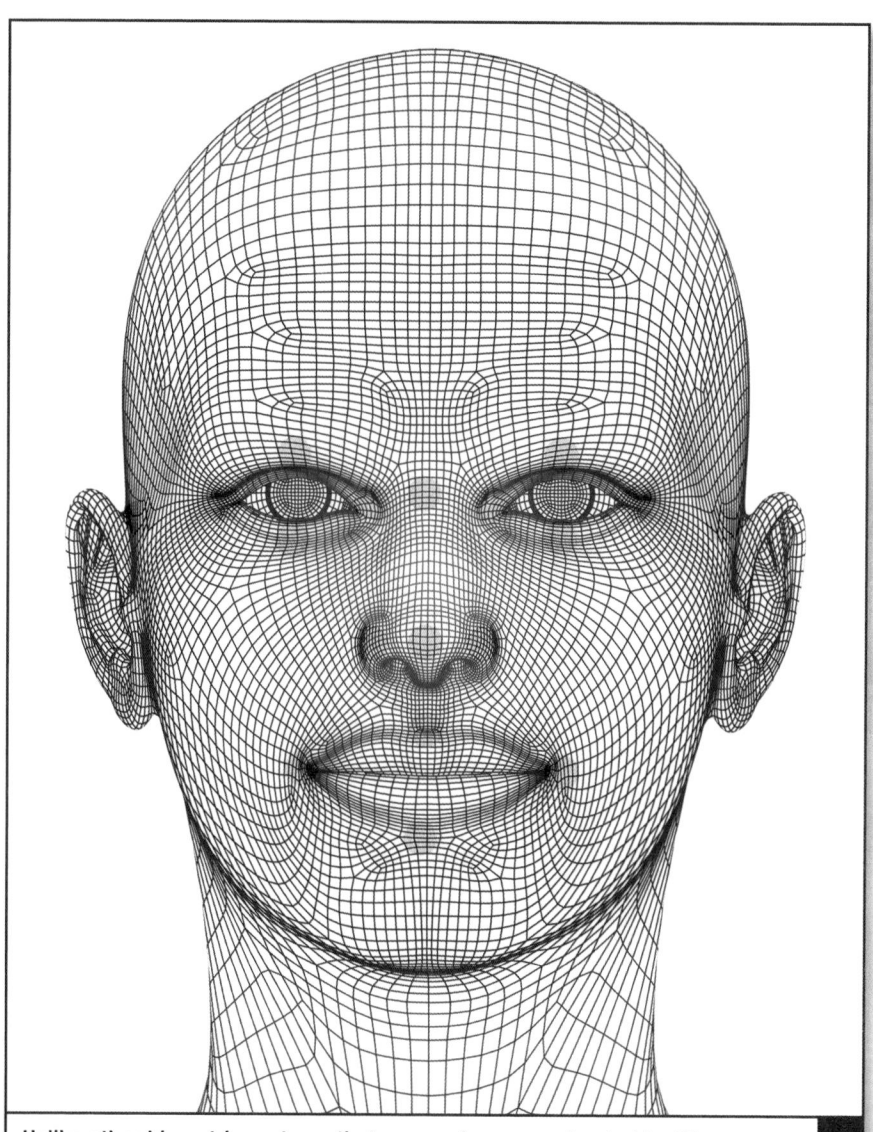

Unlike other biometric systems that scan only one marker to identify a person, facial recognition software uses a number of facial markers, referred to as the facial landscape, to identify a person.

the user's face, such as the distance between the tip of the nose and the corners of the eyes. As with fingerprint scanning, the software stores the measurements as a numeric code, known as a faceprint. A user can scan his or her face by taking a selfie or a video of the face to create the faceprint record. Then, whenever the user wants to access the protected device, he or she simply looks into the camera before touching the screen or clicking a mouse to unlock the device. The image is then compared to the faceprint on record. "Essentially what is being looked at is a landscape of the face," says Elke Oberg, marketing manager with Cognitec Systems, a facial recognition vendor. "Facial recognition software takes various measurements of each face and turns these into a string of numbers. Then it's just a matter of comparing one string of numbers with another. The higher the similarity score, the more likely it is that you're looking at the same person."[30]

One of the simplest biometric identification systems is based on the user's unique voice characteristics, a method known as voice recognition or speaker recognition. This is not to be confused with speech recognition, which focuses on the ability of a machine to "understand" a user's speech for the purpose of performing specific tasks. Personal voice assistants such as Apple's Siri, Microsoft's Cortana, Google's Google Now, and Amazon's Alexa use speech recognition to interpret instructions and perform a variety of tasks, from answering questions to opening files and sending e-mails. Speaker recognition is different. It identifies who is speaking, rather than what is being said.

Speaker recognition normally is accomplished by having the user create a voiceprint by reading words, numbers, or phrases aloud. The voice recognition software analyzes and records one hundred different measurements of attributes of the user's speech, including cadence, pronunciation, and physical qualities such as the sounds made by lips, tongue, larynx (voice box), and breathing. When users attempt to log in, they are prompted to say a few words known as a passphrase. The words themselves are not important. The software compares the sounds made by the speaker to the stored voiceprint. The identifying traits of a user's voice are present no matter what he or she says, so the passphrases can change with every log-in, and users do not have to remember any of them. Fooling the system is difficult. While some people can mimic voices very well, what they hear and reproduce is different than what the software hears, records, and matches to the voiceprint. Changes in the user's voice due to illness or overuse will not prevent a successful log-in, since many of the speech attributes, such as the cadence of the speech, are not affected by such conditions.

While voice recognition technology is not being used to unlock phones or other computing devices at this time, it is being used as a security measure in telephone banking systems. The British banks Barclays and HSBC both use voice recognition technology to verify the identity of customers using automated telephone banking, as does one of India's largest banks, ICICI Bank. "Our decision to invest in this new technology was primarily driven by the objective of enhancing convenience and the everyday banking experience of our customers,"[31] explained ICICI executive director Rajiv Sabharwal. Before adopting the voice recognition system, ICICI phone banking customers had to enter a sixteen-digit account number followed by a four-digit password to establish their identity—and they had to do it in a limited amount of time or the transaction would be dropped. Voice recognition security has eliminated that problem.

Closing the Back Door ■

As cybersecurity engineers strengthen user authentication and design other methods for safely unlocking the front door to devices and networks, they also are constantly trying to close the back door to systems by identifying and fixing vulnerabilities in firewalls, antivirus programs, and software programs. To accomplish this, technology companies create software enhancements that target identified vulnerabilities. These applications, known as security patches, can be downloaded for free or as part of a paid support package. Typically, the company issuing the security patch notifies users and tells them to download the patch. These alerts are a double-edged sword, however. Not only do they notify users and prompt them to fix the problem, they also alert hackers to a vulnerability that has been found. The hackers can download the patch, analyze it, and find out exactly what the weakness is. Hackers then have a period of time to attack the weakness before all the users respond to the alert and download the patch.

The period between the release of the security patch and its installation by the user is known as the recovery period. The longer the recovery period, the more time hackers have to exploit

Does Antivirus Software Help Hackers?

According to research firm Gartner, consumers spend about $5 billion a year on third-party antivirus software. Some computing experts believe that is too much—about $5 billion too much. "Don't buy antivirus software, and uninstall it if you already have it," writes Robert O'Callahan, a former engineer at Internet browser company Mozilla. "At best, there is negligible evidence that major non-MS [Microsoft] AV [antivirus] products give a net improvement in security. More likely, they hurt security significantly."

O'Callahan explains that because antivirus software is granted access to the deepest parts of the operating system, known as the kernel, it can open up pathways, or vectors, for hackers or malware to follow and exploit. "See [the] bugs in AV products listed in Google's Project Zero [report]," writes O'Callahan. "These bugs indicate that not only do these products open many attack vectors, but in general their developers do not follow standard security practices." In addition, some antivirus programs prevent users from updating their Internet browsers with new security patches. "Several times AV software blocked Firefox updates, making it impossible for users to receive important security fixes," writes O'Callahan. He advises home computer users to rely on their operating systems' built-in firewalls for protection.

Quoted in Tech Desk, "Anti-virus Software Is Just a Terrible Idea, Warns Former Mozilla Engineer," *Indian Express* (Mumbai, India), January 30, 2017. http://indianexpress.com.

the vulnerability. Cybersecurity experts are always searching for ways to shorten the recovery period. Research by Cisco shows that users are more likely to download security patches if they occur at regular intervals spaced well apart. For example, a Cisco study found that nearly 80 percent of Adobe Flash users installed software updates within one week of release. However, in late 2015 Adobe released five updates in rapid succession. When this occurred, the users did not keep pace, and the number of users with the latest version of the system fell dramatically. "Such a flurry of updates may confuse users," write the Cisco researchers. "They may question whether they need to download so many updates; they can become fatigued by the number of upgrade notifications; and they may think they've already downloaded a crucial update and can ignore new notifications. No matter what drives their lack of interest in installing an update, it's bad news for defenders."[32]

To overcome user fatigue, confusion, or disinterest, cybersecurity experts created a way for software updates to occur automatically, without the user having to download them. Automatic software updates usually occur when the user attempts to power off the device. The user might be asked to keep the power on until the updates have finished loading. The system then powers off by itself once the updates are completed. With automatic updates, the recovery period usually is less than one day, since most people power off their devices at night.

Foiling Physical Intruders ■

Even with 2FA and up-to-date security patches in place, a physical intruder who steals both a user's laptop and smartphone usually can open the devices, learn a user's passwords, and gain access to multiple accounts. Engineers have come up with ways to address this security problem as well. The solutions generally are known as "Find My" applications, named after Apple's original Find My iPhone application. Find My applications have been created not only for Apple products such as iPad tablets and MacBook laptop computers, but for virtually any smartphone or computer, provided they have been loaded with the proper software at the factory or by the user. Find My programs allow the user to track the location of the missing device on an online map, lock the device remotely, and even erase all its data so that even if the hacker manages to break in, there is nothing to find.

With Apple products, the Find My function is built in at the factory and cannot be removed. Even if the thief performs a factory reset on the device, the owner can still track the location of the device and remotely manage it. As soon as the user realizes the device is missing, he or she can log in to Apple's iCloud website and register the device as lost. After putting the device in "lost mode," the user can see not only where the device is, but also where it has been. This can help the user decide if the device is simply lost or has been stolen. The user can then make an informed decision about what action to take. To ensure that the person who has the phone cannot access any personal data, the user can enter a four-digit passcode to lock the device. Once this is in place, no one can open the device without the passcode. The user can also send a message to the locked screen of the device. The message can contain contact information, so the person who found the device can contact the owner.

Although the number of hackers, malware, and cyberattacks are growing at an alarming rate, technologies such as 2FA, biometric identification, automatic software updates, and remote locking of lost or stolen devices are tightening security for individual devices and online accounts. Wider adoption of these cutting-edge technologies will greatly reduce the number of successful attacks on individuals.

CHAPTER 4

SOLUTIONS: Improving Network Security

"Every day, cyber attacks become more sophisticated and harder to defeat. Because of this ongoing development, we cannot tell exactly what kind of threats will emerge next year, in five years' time, or in ten years' time; we can only say that these threats will be even more dangerous than those of today."

—Ken Allan, global security leader at financial services company EY

Ken Allan et al., *Cybersecurity and the Internet of Things*. London: EY, p. 10. www.ey.com.

Cybersecurity engineers have made great progress in securing individual devices and user accounts, but large computer networks and data centers pose even greater challenges. This is because hackers often can find more points to attack in a large network, and they have more time to do it since the systems often run around the clock. As a result, network cybersecurity has many facets—securing users, building better firewalls, cutting down the amount of time hackers have to compromise the system after gaining access, and encrypting data so it is useless even if it is stolen. As the frequency of cyberattacks increases, more organizations will find it necessary to adopt these advanced solutions.

Establishing Trust ■

One method of improving cybersecurity is to better verify the identity of people using the network, as well as the identity of users' devices and individuals' authority to access the system. The process of using multiple layers of identification is sometimes called establishing trust. For example, a trust system might require 2FA before allowing a user to access a network, just as traditional systems do now. However, it might also require the user to verify the identity of the device being used to access the network, again through two-factor identification or perhaps biometric identification. With both the identity of the user and the device established, the system might further require identification during the transaction, whether that is transferring a file or using a particular software program, such as a document management system. "Enterprise security used to mean building a wall of protection around an organization to keep out the bad guys," explains T. Kendall Hunt, chair and chief executive officer of VASCO Digital Security. "Now, establishing trust in the highly interactive, digital world requires scalable user and transaction-centric security approaches that work together to ensure trusted identities, trusted devices, trusted channels, and trusted transactions."[33]

Penetration Testing ■

One of the first techniques cybersecurity experts use to improve the security of a system is to stage mock attacks to identify weaknesses. This is called penetration testing, or pentesting. Penetration testing is arranged by the organization, but it is often conducted without the knowledge of the organization's security analysts or network administrators. Like a hacker, the penetration tester probes for weaknesses in the network, examining ports and testing passwords. After completing the analysis, the pentester provides a written report of all of a system's vulnerabilities so they can be secured.

Once a pentester has broken into a system, the even more important work begins. The pentester tries to establish how long it takes for the existing security system to detect the security breach. The reaction time of the security staff is critical. Fast reaction time reduces the amount of time a real hacker is allowed to roam free through the system. This period of time is known as the "time to detection" or "dwell time."

In a June 2016 survey, the SANS Institute asked 591 security professionals to estimate their dwell times. Twenty-eight percent said they could detect a security breach within the first twenty-four hours after it occurred. Seventeen percent said they could discover the breach within twenty-four to forty-eight hours. The rest—45 percent of the respondents—said it would take them more than two days to learn of the incident. Fully 20 percent admitted it would take more than one month before they knew they had been hacked. The SANS survey actually shows an improvement in time to detection. According to a 2015 survey of 844 security practitioners by the Ponemon Institute, it took an average of 98 days for financial services companies to detect a breach of their security and 197 days for retail companies to do so. Though time to detection has improved slightly, "the time to detect an advanced threat is far too long," says Larry Ponemon, chair and founder of the Ponemon Institute. "Attackers are getting in and staying long enough that the damage caused is often irreparable."[34]

Cybersecurity staff must react quickly when a breach is detected. The faster their reaction, the less time a hacker has to roam around in the system.

Pentesters usually do not recommend solutions; they only probe the systems for weaknesses. However, solutions to reduce dwell time do exist. These include host intrusion detection (HID) and network intrusion detection (NID) systems. These systems are constantly being refined so they can detect intruders more quickly. Most HID systems monitor the file activity on a computer. The system notes which files are being opened, copied, moved, or deleted. If the system detects something unusual, known as an anomaly, it alerts the user or a network administrator and asks for confirmation that the file activity is authorized. Most NID systems monitor activity levels of a network. They scan packets of data for malware and also watch for unusual behavior, such as large amounts of data being exported from the system. These systems are often programmed with unchanging rules, or parameters. However, researchers are now working on ways to make the systems more precise and effective using technology known as machine learning.

Machine learning is a type of artificial intelligence that allows computers to analyze data and make decisions about it without being told by an algorithm exactly what to look for or to do. Instead, the machine "learns," or is trained, by observing normal "behavior" of digital data, such as network activity. The machine learning program is then exposed to new data, and it uses its built-in logic to analyze and make decisions about the data. For example, a machine learning system used for network security might monitor network activity over a period of time. It learns about levels of activity by area of the network, time of day, and even day of the week or day of the month. It also can note the typical sequence of requests a user makes from a server and the amount of time between the requests, allowing the system to know what is "normal." It can examine these behaviors in finer detail than a normal network intrusion program can, allowing it to identify unusual network behavior that a traditional system might miss.

The longer the machine learning is in place, the better it becomes at doing its job, because it is constantly adding to its

> **WORDS IN CONTEXT**
>
> **algorithm**
>
> a set of steps or operations that are followed in order to solve a mathematical problem or to complete a computer process

knowledge of how the network normally behaves. The system can be enhanced with predictive software that further increases its accuracy. The predictive software allows the system to take various pieces of information and translate them into expected network behavior. For example, the system might notice that a rise in activity in the help desk area of a company is often followed by increased levels of e-mail, messaging, or file transfers with another part of the company, such as product engineering. When the system detects the increased help desk activity, it will automatically anticipate the other changes. If they do not happen, the system might conclude that something is wrong and issue a security alert.

Hosted Desktops ■

Cybersecurity has become such a major concern for some organizations that they are embracing a model of networked computing that eliminates many of the security problems of a traditional computing environment: hosted desktops (HDs). From the user's point of view, an HD appears and functions exactly like the desktop of a local PC connected to a network. For example, if an organization uses Microsoft Windows, the user's desktop would display the typical Windows toolbars, start buttons, and icons in the usual places. If the user clicks on an application, it opens. However, the operating system and software applications are not installed on the user's local computer. Instead, they reside on remote servers located far away in a network of connected servers known as the cloud. What the user is interacting with is a simulated, or virtual, desktop. In fact, the user's computer might not be a PC at all but a thin client, a small computer with enough memory to support virtualization but with no hard drive and no local storage.

When the user clicks an icon to open a program, that request is sent via the Internet to a server in the cloud. The server then opens the application and sends an image of the new screen back to the user. This happens in approximately the same amount of time it would take to open an application from a local hard drive, so the user does not notice any difference. The same is true when the user types a letter or number: The thin client sends a packet of data requesting the letter to the remote server, which

Large computer centers like this one provide cloud computing. Users access the cloud for data and applications that traditionally have been stored on their own computer or local network but that are safer from hackers when accessed on the cloud.

responds with a packet of data that represents the letter on the user's screen. This is essentially how any Internet chat program works. The application that makes words appear on the screen is not running on the local computer, but far away on a server in the cloud. From the user's point of view, everything looks exactly as it would with the traditional computing network model.

Hackers Target Talking Toys

In February 2017 cybersecurity researcher Troy Hunt revealed that a database linked to plush toys called CloudPets was vulnerable to cyberattacks. His revelation showed the growing threat posed by the IoE. CloudPets are toy animals that enable people to send voice greetings to children via the toy, using a smartphone app. Hunt wrote that he had gained access to 820,000 CloudPet user accounts defended with extremely weak passwords, some containing only one letter. "Because there were no rules, lots of people created bad passwords," Hunt said. "I did an exercise and found it was really easy to create them. Lots of people were using the password Cloudpets because that's what people do." Another of the toy's weaknesses is that it does not require any kind of authentication to synchronize it with other digital devices, such as smartphones, tablets, or PCs. Such devices are often linked on a home computer network using a wireless router. Hackers with access to the toy could then connect to other devices on the home network, stealing files, passwords, and personal information such as Social Security numbers. "If you have a CloudPets bear, switch it off," advises security researcher Ken Munro. "It might be a good idea for people to try to delete their accounts. . . . Try to remember what password you set for the account—and if you used it anywhere else, change it."

Quoted in BBC, "Children's Messages in CloudPets Data Breach," February 28, 2017. www.bbc.com.

From a security point of view, however, everything is different with an HD. First, the operating system is always current, since the provider of the HD installs all updates as soon as they are released. The HD provider is able to do this because offering the software as a service is the company's business and its primary focus. All software is fully up-to-date as well, and all security patches are implemented immediately. This eliminates the issue of malware or a hacker exploiting a known security weakness.

HD systems are immune to physical intruders as well, since all of the organization's data is stored on remote servers and nothing is stored locally on the user's thin client. Even if a hacker manages to penetrate the user's office and steal a thin client, the device contains no data and no software the hacker can use to gain entrance to the organization's system. Hackers cannot gain physical access to the organization's servers, either, since they are located far away, in the HD provider's data center. These facilities are more like a bank vault than a business location. Only a small number of people are allowed access to the HD servers, and they must pass through robust security systems such as biometric scanning.

Whitelisting ■

Computer systems can also be safeguarded against internal security threats, intruders, or hackers who manage to defeat the 2FA system by using a technique known as whitelisting. With this process, users are only allowed to open software that applies to their work. If the user is not approved, or whitelisted, to use an application, it will not open. Each user who is whitelisted is assigned a unique digital code, or signature, for each approved application. The digital signature must match the one on record for the application to run. This stops unauthorized users—both internal and external—from opening or running unauthorized applications. It prevents malware from operating as well. For example, malware might be received as an attachment to an e-mail and appear to be a Microsoft Word document, but it is actually an executable file. When the user clicks on the attachment, it might try to open directly, or it might prompt the user to confirm that he or she wants to open it. There is every chance the user would indeed click "Yes" to open the attachment. However, since the malware lacks the required digital signature to run that application, it is not allowed to execute. This is true for any malicious program a user might download from the Internet, attempt to install, or receive in an e-mail. "Whitelisting can be far more effective than an antivirus program," says Simon Ponsford, chief executive officer of Cranberry Cloud, an HD provider. He explains:

> Antivirus programs examine the suspicious file, looking for strings of known malicious code, also known as definitions. With new malware being constantly created, an antivirus

program can fail to detect malicious code that has not yet been identified, or defined, in the latest release of the antivirus software. With whitelisting, it doesn't matter if the malware is detected or not. If a user, hacker, or system attempts to execute an application that is not approved, that is, if the application's digital signature, does not match the whitelist, and is not located in a pre-defined path, it cannot execute. Rather than "blacklisting" forbidden programs and allowing everything else to run, whitelisting requires a positive match for the program to execute. Just because a program does not turn up on a blacklist, that does not mean it will be allowed to run. Its digital signature must match the whitelist.[35]

Whitelisting is not unique to HDs. For example, Microsoft offers an option called AppLocker for its Windows operating system for businesses. AppLocker allows the administrator (and not the user) to select, or whitelist, which applications will run on a particular computer.

With an HD system, everything the user does must travel over the Internet to the remote servers and then back to the virtual desktop. This gives hackers an opportunity to intercept the data somewhere along the line. This is because data sent over the Internet does not follow a straight line but is switched from various servers along the way to make the most efficient use of the Internet bandwidth. For example, the data packet containing the first letter of a word might be sent from a server to one switching station, known as an Internet router, while the data packet containing the second letter of the word might be sent to another Internet router. The packets are reassembled in the right order at the other end of the Internet connection. However, all packets must go through the local router at each end. HD providers often cloak, or hide, the IP addresses of their servers, so hackers cannot determine which router the provider is using.

To prevent hackers from obtaining useful information in the event that they are able to intercept transmissions, HD providers use software to encrypt the data, transforming it into a secret code. Encrypted data is almost impossible for hackers to read.

Encryption ■

Encryption is not limited to an HD or virtual environment. A growing number of organizations with traditional networks are encrypting the data stored on their servers and traveling over their networks. Of all the security measures being used today, encryption holds the most promise for preventing hackers from obtaining valuable information. "The hackers will continue to be inventive in their ways to infiltrate our data but the progress in computing power, even at the consumer level, means ever increasing complexity in encryption algorithms and thus the good guys staying ahead of the bad guys,"[36] says Richard Hancock, a data protection officer at GlobalSign, a provider of identity verification systems.

Most security measures are aimed at stopping hackers from gaining access to data. Encryption is different; it assumes the hackers already have the data. Jason Schwent and Fredric Roth, attorneys who specialize in cybersecurity compliance in the legal profession, explain the need for encryption this way:

> With the increased rate of data breaches targeting personal information, an increased public awareness of online privacy, and an increasingly demanding regulatory landscape, large and small businesses are looking to additional forms of security to protect themselves and their customers from unauthorized access. These efforts have largely targeted preventing unauthorized access via different types of access control, like firewalls, strong passwords, anti-malware, two-factor authentication and data sandboxing. However, businesses must also plan for the failure of these technologies. In the event that unauthorized individuals gain access to sensitive data, businesses are increasingly turning to data encryption to safeguard the data itself.[37]

Encryption is designed to prevent hackers from understanding the data they have accessed. It does this by scrambling the binary code—the ones and zeroes that make up digital data—in such a way that the data is unreadable. The only way to make sense of the scrambled data is to unscramble it using the correct

How Data Is Encrypted

Data encryption is an increasingly common way for individuals and companies to prevent hackers from obtaining valuable information. Encryption scrambles data so that a hacker cannot read it. The only way to make sense of scrambled data is to unscramble it using a key—a complex algorithm, or set of instructions performed by a computer. There are two types of encryption: symmetric-key encryption and asymmetric-key encryption. Symmetric-key encryption is commonly used for confidential online communications, e-mail messages, and document files. Asymmetric-key encryption is commonly used for intranet and Internet functions.

Symmetric-Key Encryption

In symmetric-key encryption, both the sender and the receiver (and only the sender and receiver) possess the same secret key. That key is used to encrypt readable plaintext, which becomes unreadable ciphertext. It then decrypts the ciphertext, so that it once again becomes readable plaintext. Since both users have the same key, this method is known as symmetric-key encryption.

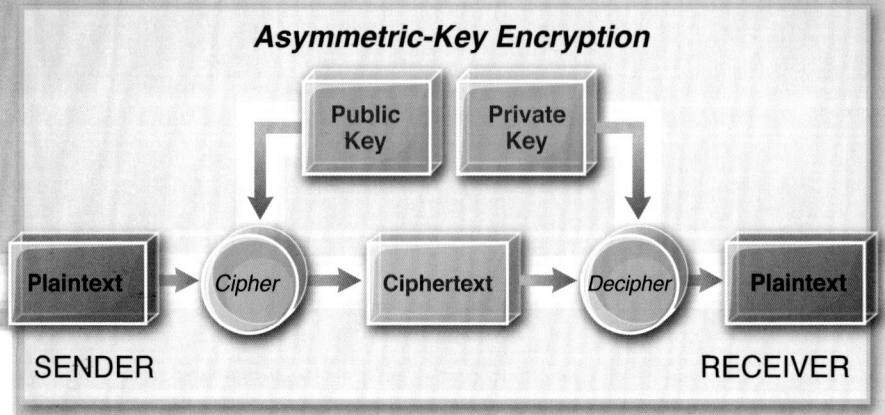

Asymmetric-Key Encryption

In asymmetric-key encryption, any number of senders can use a public key to encrypt plaintext. The resulting ciphertext is unreadable to everyone except for the recipient. The recipient (and only the recipient) has a private key that is paired with the public key. The private key can be used to decipher any ciphertext generated using the paired public key. This eliminates the need for both the sender and the recipient to always have matching keys. Since users do not have matching keys, this method is known as asymmetric-key encryption.

Source: Spanish Scientific Research Council, "Intypedia: Information Security Encyclopedia," 2010. www.criptored.upm.es.

method, or key. In data encryption, the key is not known by any person; it is a complex algorithm, or set of instructions performed by a computer.

The encryption key is not accessible through the network, where hackers could find it. Instead, it often is embedded in a piece of hardware that only certain authorized users have. The key can also be a software program only certain users can access. To use the encryption key, the user often must sign in using 2FA. As a result, hackers who have managed to gain access to a network are unable to access the encryption key without being physically present or having obtained a user's verification device, such as a smartphone or dongle.

Encryption Becomes a Requirement ■

Data encryption is becoming a requirement in some industries. For example, the US Department of Health and Human Services has enacted rules under a federal law known as the Health Insurance Portability and Accountability Act (HIPAA) that require medical organizations to use a number of technologies, including data encryption, to safeguard patient medical records. The HIPAA security rule provides examples of encryption methods that can be used. In addition, the HIPAA Omnibus Rule of 2013 holds medical organizations legally liable for failing to comply with the HIPAA Security Rule.

Similarly, the American Bar Association (ABA), a professional association of lawyers and law students, recently updated its ABA Model Rule 1.1 with a requirement that an attorney keep up-to-date with security technology. "The duty to stay abreast of changes in the law and practice includes understanding the benefits and risks of relevant technology,"[38] states the ABA. Although not a law, the rule suggests that attorneys who do not encrypt privileged client data could be successfully sued for failing to comply with their professional responsibilities.

Many banks and financial services companies already encrypt the data they send over networks. "Finance houses will no longer see database encryption as optional and you would expect the industry leaders to drive these best practices forward to make it a standard,"[39] says Hancock. Some European banks have begun to use a next-generation form of encryption known as quantum key

Microsoft Deploys Machine Learning to Bolster Security

In addition to developing and selling computer software, consumer electronics, and PCs, Microsoft Corporation also offers cloud computing services. Cloud computing services provide large clusters of interconnected computers for companies to use to run software and store data. To improve the security of the Microsoft cloud, the company deployed a machine learning system capable of processing 10 terabytes (10 trillion bytes) of data every day. The machine learning system observes activity on the global network and uses the data to create a security graph to help protect its customers. "The intelligent security graph is our attempt to collect trillions of signals from billions of data sources so that we can triangulate what the bad guys are doing and where they're at," says Tim Rains, chief security advisor at Microsoft. Among other things, the system analyzes the locations of log-in attempts. Microsoft learned that almost three-quarters of the log-in attempts came from places where the valid user had either rarely or never logged in, indicating the activity of hackers. "The reason we use machine learning is because there's no way humans can actually aggregate and analyze that much security data, day in and day out, there's just too much of it," explains Rains.

Quoted in Michael Hill, "Microsoft Using Machine Learning to Strengthen Security," *Infosecurity Magazine*, May 5, 2016. www.infosecurity-magazine.com.

distribution (QKD) to secure their financial transactions. With this technology, encryption keys are sent over fiber-optic networks using photons of light. Although the keys can be intercepted, they cannot be copied and sent on without changing them slightly. As a result, the entity receiving the photons can immediately tell if the key has been tampered with. "By comparing measurements of the properties of a fraction of these photons, it's possible to show that no eavesdropper is listening in and that the keys are thus safe to use; this is what we mean by 'provably secure,'"[40] writes security expert Don Hayford.

Although largely effective at making information unreadable by hackers, encryption does have drawbacks. The encrypting and decrypting of a piece, or bit, of data requires additional computing power, consuming more energy than the processing of unencrypted data does. Encryption and decryption also take time. Organizations that decide to encrypt their data may need to invest in newer, faster hardware to keep the data flowing at a high rate. This is especially true when an organization decides to encrypt an entire database containing huge amounts of data. Advanced systems such as QKDs are extremely expensive, which so far is limiting their use. "While products based on QKD already are being used by banks and governments in Europe—especially Switzerland—they have not been deployed commercially in the United States to any great extent,"[41] writes Hayford.

Another potential issue is incorrect data storage. For example, a person receiving an encrypted file from a server might decrypt it and then save it on the local hard drive. Schwent and Roth write:

> Encryption systems are also vulnerable to inconsistent application. When encrypted data is sent between systems, it may be encrypted when created and when transmitted, but once it reaches its destination, it may be stored in an unencrypted format, unbeknownst to the sender. When employing an encryption system to protect data that is shared with or received from other entities, it is important to understand where the encryption begins and where it ends.[42]

One of the benefits of an organization using thin clients instead of PCs is that thin clients are not capable of storing unencrypted data locally, where hackers or internal threats can access it. All data is stored on servers, whether remote or local, where it is automatically reencrypted when it is saved.

Data encryption by itself cannot solve all cybersecurity issues, because it still depends on the correct person receiving and using the decryption key. Currently, users receiving an encryption key establish their identity using standard user account access controls, such as passwords, passphrases, 2FA, and biometrics. If these systems are not strong, hackers can gain access to the encrypted data. "As with any digital security system, the weakest link is often the human user," write Schwent and Roth. "Thus, it is important to remember that encryption can only be a single part of a more comprehensive and multi-part security system employed to protect data."[43]

As long as hackers believe they can make money quickly and easily by hacking, they will continue to do so—in ever-increasing numbers. No single technology can stop all cyberattacks, but defenders can deploy an array of advanced technologies to reduce the vulnerabilities that hackers exploit, limit the time they have to do damage, and make it too time consuming and too expensive for them to decode encrypted data. For now, the goal of cybersecurity experts is simply to raise the cost of attacking the system they are defending so that hackers move on to more inviting targets.

SOURCE NOTES

INTRODUCTION
A Growing Concern

1. Michael D. Shear and Matthew Rosenberg, "Released Emails Suggest the D.N.C. Derided the Sanders Campaign," *New York Times*, July 22, 2016. www.nytimes.com.
2. Kaveh Waddell, "Why Some People Think a Typo Cost Clinton the Election," *Atlantic*, December 16, 2016. www.theatlantic.com.
3. Harry Enten, "How Much Did Wikileaks Hurt Hillary Clinton?," FiveThirtyEight, December 23, 2016. https://fivethirtyeight.com.
4. Quoted in Allen Cone, "U.S. punishes Russia for Alleged Election Hacking with Sanctions, Expulsion of Diplomats," UPI, December 29, 2016. www.upi.com.
5. Barack Obama, "Remarks by the President in Final Press Conference," The White House, Office of the Press Secretary, January 18, 2017. https://obamawhitehouse.archives.gov.
6. Quoted in Dan Tynan, "The State of Cyber Security: We're All Screwed," *Guardian* (Manchester), August 8, 2016. www.theguardian.com.

CHAPTER 1
CURRENT STATUS: Layers of Cybersecurity Defense

7. David Pogue, "Remember All Those Passwords? No Need," *New York Times*, June 5, 2013. www.nytimes.com.
8. Pogue, "Remember All Those Passwords? No Need."
9. Quoted in Tynan, "The State of Cyber Security."
10. Cisco Systems Inc., *Cisco 2017 Annual Cybersecurity Report.* San Jose, CA: Cisco Systems, 2017, p. 53.
11. Quoted in Kenneth Corbin, "Cybersecurity Pros in High Demand, Highly Paid and Highly Selective," CIO.com, August 8, 2013. www.cio.com.

CHAPTER 2
PROBLEMS: Weaknesses Exploited by Hackers

12. Verizon, *Verizon 2016 Data Breach Investigations Report*. New York: Verizon, 2016, p. 29.
13. Webroot, "2017 Webroot Threat Report Reveals Dramatic Increase in Technology Company Phishing Attacks—Seven Times More Likely than Financial Institutions," February 13, 2017. www.webroot.com.
14. Quoted in Ryan Francis, "Hospital Devices Left Vulnerable, Leave Patients at Risk," CIO.com, February 9, 2017. www.cio.com.
15. Quoted in Francis, "Hospital Devices Left Vulnerable, Leave Patients at Risk."
16. Cisco Systems Inc., *Cisco 2017 Annual Cybersecurity Report*, p. 10.
17. Quoted in Lorenzo Franceschi-Bicchierai, "A Whole Lot of Nitwits Will Plug a Random USB into Their Computer, Study Finds," Motherboard, April 6, 2016. https://motherboard.vice.com.
18. Matthew Tischer et al., "Users Really Do Plug In USB Drives They Find," paper presented at the Thirty-Seventh IEEE Symposium on Security and Privacy, San Jose, CA, May 2016.
19. Verizon, *Verizon 2016 Data Breach Investigations Report*, p. 18.
20. Cisco Systems Inc., *Cisco 2017 Annual Cybersecurity Report*, p. 10.
21. Jurijs Girtakovskis et al., *2017 Webroot Threat Report*. Broomfield, CO: Webroot, 2017, p. 13. https://webroot-cms-cdn.s3.amazonaws.com.
22. Fred McClimans et al., *The State of Cybersecurity and Digital Trust 2016*. Cambridge, MA: Accenture and HfS Research, 2016, p. 9. www.accenture.com.
23. Quoted in Zack Whittaker, "How Did One Contractor Steal 50TB of NSA Data? Easily, Say Former Spies," ZDNet, October 28, 2016. www.zdnet.com.
24. Quoted in Michael Cooney, "Yikes: 10,000 IRS Impersonation Scam Calls Are Placed Every Week," *Network World*, April 15, 2015. www.networkworld.com.

25. Cisco Systems Inc., *Cisco 2017 Annual Cybersecurity Report*, p. 3.

CHAPTER 3
SOLUTIONS: Strengthening Personal Identification

26. Apple, "About Touch ID Security on iPhone and iPad," 2017. https://support.apple.com.
27. Apple, "About Touch ID Security on iPhone and iPad."
28. Quoted in April Glaser, "Biometrics Are Coming, Along with Serious Security Concerns," *Wired*, March 9, 2016. www.wired,com.
29. Quoted in Planet Biometics, "Qatar National Bank Adds Iris ID Tech to ATMs," December 14, 2016. www.planetbiometrics.com.
30. Quoted in Consumer Reports, "How Facial Recognition Works: The Ghost in the Camera," January 4, 2016. www.consumerreports.org.
31. Quoted in *Business Today*, "ICICI Eyes 5 Million Transactions via Voice-Recognition," September 25, 2016. www.businesstoday.in.
32. Cisco Systems Inc., *Cisco 2017 Annual Cybersecurity Report*, p. 46.

CHAPTER 4
SOLUTIONS: Improving Network Security

33. T. Kendall Hunt, "VASCO Delivers Trust-Centric Security at RSA," video, Vasco Digital Security. www.vasco.com.
34. Quoted in Charlie Osborne, "Most Companies Take over Six Months to Detect Data Breaches," ZDNet, May 19, 2015. www.zdnet.com.
35. Simon Ponsford, interview with the author, March 6, 2017.
36. Richard Hancock, "The Future of Cybersecurity: Predictions from GlobalSign," *GlobalSign Blog*, GlobalSign, October 28, 2016. www.globalsign.com.
37. Jason Schwent and Fredric Roth, "Is Encryption the Key to Your Data Security?," *Cybersecurity Bits and Bytes* (blog), Thompson Coburn, August 9, 2016. www.thompsoncoburn.com.

38. Quoted in Schwent and Roth, "Is Encryption the Key to Your Data Security?"

39. Hancock, "The Future of Cybersecurity."

40. Don Hayford, "The Future of Security: Zeroing In on Unhackable Data with Quantum Key Distribution," *Wired*, September 2014. www.wired.com.

41. Hayford, "The Future of Security."

42. Schwent and Roth, "Is Encryption the Key to Your Data Security?"

43. Schwent and Roth, "Is Encryption the Key to Your Data Security?"

FIND OUT MORE

Books
Margaret J. Goldstein and Martin Gitlin, *Cyber Attack*. Minneapolis, MN: Twenty-First Century, 2015.

Marc Goodman, *Future Crimes: Inside the Digital Underground and the Battle for Our Connected World*. New York: Anchor, 2016.

Raef Meeuwisse, *Cybersecurity for Beginners*. 2nd ed. Hythe, England: Cyber Simplicity, 2017.

Bruce Schneier, *Data and Goliath: The Hidden Battles to Collect Your Data and Control Your World*. New York: Norton, 2015.

P.W. Singer and Allan Friedman, *Cybersecurity and Cyberwar: What Everyone Needs to Know*. Oxford: Oxford University Press, 2014.

Websites
Hacker Highschool—Security Awareness for Teens (www .hackerhighschool.org). The nonprofit Institute for Security and Open Methodologies offers eleven downloadable, hands-on lessons designed for self-guided learning by teens on the topics of hacking and cybersecurity. Lessons include "Being a Hacker," "Essential Commands," "Hacking Malware," "Attack Analysis," "Forensics," and more.

NAE Grand Challenges for Engineering (www.engineeringcha llenges.org). Created by the National Academy of Engineering, this website offers a list of the grand challenges and opportunities for engineering facing those born at the dawn of this century, including a section called "Securing Cyberspace."

Stay Safe Online (www.staysafeonline.org). The National Cyber Security Alliance, a nonprofit organization devoted to educating people about how to use the Internet safely and securely, features web pages for teens such as "Malware & Botnets," "Spam & Phishing," "Hacked Accounts," and "Securing Your Home Network."

US Department of Homeland Security (www.dhs.gov/topic /cybersecurity). The US Department of Homeland Security offers news and information on a range of cybersecurity topics. The website includes articles such as "Combating Cyber Crime," "Cyber Safety," "Cybersecurity Jobs," "Cybersecurity Training & Exercises," "Education," and "What You Can Do."

Internet Sources

Jurijs Girtakovskis et al., *2017 Webroot Threat Report*. Broomfield, CO: Webroot, 2017. https://webroot-cms-cdn.s3.amazonaws .com/8114/8667/3161/Webroot_2017_Threat_Report_US.pdf.

Richard Hancock, "The Future of Cybersecurity: Predictions from GlobalSign," *GlobalSign Blog*, GlobalSign, October 28, 2016. www.globalsign.com/en/blog/future-of-cybersecurity.

Fred McClimans et al., *The State of Cybersecurity and Digital Trust 2016*. Cambridge, MA: Accenture and HfS Research, 2016. www.accenture.com/t20160704T014005__w__/us-en/_acnme dia/PDF-23/Accenture-State-Cybersecurity-and-Digital-Trust -2016-Report-June.pdf.

INDEX

PICTURE CREDITS

ABOUT THE AUTHOR

Bradley Steffens is an award-winning poet, playwright, novelist, and author of more than thirty-five nonfiction books for children and young adults. He is a two-time recipient of the San Diego Book Award for Best Young Adult and Children's Nonfiction: His *Giants* won the 2005 award, and his *J.K. Rowling* claimed the 2007 prize. Steffens also received the Theodor S. Geisel Award for best book by a San Diego County author in 2007.